JB JOSSEY-BASS™
A Wiley Brand

All About Sponsorships

SECOND EDITION

Scott C. Stevenson, Editor

WILEY

978-1-118-69037-6   ISBN

978-1-118-70393-9   ISBN (online)

All About Sponsorships
— 2nd Edition

Published by

Stevenson, Inc.

P.O. Box 4528 • Sioux City, Iowa • 51104

Phone 712.239.3010 • Fax 712.239.2166

www.stevensoninc.com

TABLE OF CONTENTS

All About Sponsorships, Second Edition.
Edited by Scott C. Stevenson.
© 2012 Stevenson, Inc. Published 2012 by Stevenson, Inc.

SETTING THE SPONSORSHIP STAGE

Six Reasons to Have Sponsorship Guidelines in Place

Do you have sponsorship guidelines? There are several reasons why having them makes good sense.

Sponsorship guidelines are like New Year's resolutions. They sound like a good idea, but they require time, energy and commitment to put in place and follow. But that shouldn't prevent you from putting sponsorship guidelines in place, says Tim Griswold, executive director and founder, Foundation for Caregivers (Chantilly, VA).

"I come from the for-profit world (where I) saw published guidelines to be as logical as having published service policies for a business," Griswold says. When he moved into the nonprofit world, he says, "I found the absence of guidelines to be quite surprising."

So Griswold and board member Mary Madsen started creating policies that would make them accountable for what they were saying and let prospective sponsors know what the Foundation for Caregivers stood for and represented.

The process has been educational, says Griswold, who shares six reasons why sponsorship guidelines are worth having:

1. **They simplify communications.** When communicating with prospective sponsors you point them to your guidelines.

2. **Sponsorship guidelines keep you honest.** It is easy to compromise your standards if you are the only one who knows those standards. When you post them for everyone to read it makes it really difficult to take shortcuts.

3. **Sponsorship guidelines convey professionalism.** If your organization is just starting out, guidelines let people know you are serious.

4. **Sponsorship guidelines force clarity.** The process of writing the guidelines forces you to make sure you don't mislead or paint your way into a corner.

5. **Sponsorship guidelines force you to work through the details.** Setting guidelines will require you to address questions or issues you may have glossed over or left until a later date.

6. **Sponsorship guidelines inform sponsors.** Guidelines let them know you are aware of risks associated with sponsorship and what you are trying to do to mitigate those risks.

View the foundation's sponsorship guidelines at: www.ffcg.org/sponsorship.htm

Source: Tim Griswold, Executive Director and Founder, Foundation for Caregivers, Caldwell, ID. . E-mail: tgriswold@ffcg.org

Questions Help Develop Sponsorship Guidelines

Tim Griswold, executive director and founder, Foundation for Caregivers (Chantilly, VA), says sponsorship guidelines are a great way to clarify your organization's stance on fundraising partnerships. But what should you consider when you are creating sponsorship guidelines for your organization?

Asking yourself these questions will provide you a step in the right direction:

❑ What are your organization's core beliefs?

❑ What should be covered? How detailed should you get?

❑ What are you seeking sponsorship for?

❑ What are your fundraising goals?

❑ Who would you like to partner with? Is there anyone you would not partner with? Why? How will you convey that?

❑ Do certain sponsors represent conflicts of interest or even the perception of a conflict of interest?

❑ Will you offer category exclusivity to certain types of businesses?

❑ Will sponsors have any say in program content or collateral materials?

❑ What benefits will sponsors receive? What responsibilities will they have?

❑ Are there any risks associated with sponsorship? If so, how are you minimizing the risks?

Form an Ongoing Sponsorship Committee

If your organization realizes significant sponsorship revenue during the course of a year — or if the potential of sponsorship revenue is great — it would be well worth your time to establish an ongoing sponsorship committee that will provide assistance and give this subject the attention it deserves.

Your sponsorship committee's roles and responsibilities may include the following:

1. To develop and submit a sponsorship policy for board approval.

2. To regularly review sponsorship benefits and make needed changes.

3. To regularly identify, research, cultivate and approach prospects for sponsorship support.

4. To assist in stewarding — and retaining — existing sponsors.

5. To be present at events and programs that have been underwritten by sponsors.

6. To review and provide input regarding all printed materials related to sponsorships.

7. To generally promote sponsorship opportunities to the public when the opportunity presents itself.

8. To assist in reviewing proposals and offering input when called on to do so.

9. To assist in evaluating each year's sponsorships and appropriately determine changes that will enhance the program over time.

When developing committees for your next special event or project, establish a sponsorship committee. Outlining the committee's goals and responsibilities will ensure that everyone is on the same page.

Observe Businesses' Marketing Behavior

How are area companies allocating their advertising dollars? What messages are they attempting to convey? What media outlets are they using?

By paying closer attention to the ways in which businesses attempt to reach the consumer, you can better match sponsorship opportunities with appropriate businesses. Equally important, by paying attention to businesses' marketing behavior, you are in a better position to identify those sponsorship benefits that best meet a particular business' wants and needs.

Work to Land First-time Gifts From Businesses

Want to get more sponsorship support from members of the business community? Create opportunities designed to get them on board. To secure more first-time gifts and sponsorships from businesses:

1. **Share a menu of wide-ranging sponsorship opportunities.** Offer a variety of sponsorship price tags.

2. **Launch a business partners program** that includes any business contributing $250 or more per year. Offer members some exclusive benefits to attract their participation.

3. **Form a committee of existing business contributors** to assist in identifying and calling on their colleagues.

4. **Convince an existing business donor to establish a challenge gift** aimed at non-donor businesses. Any first-time gift will be matched by the challenger.

Sponsorship or Philanthropy: What's the Difference

Should sponsorship be considered philanthropy? Not usually.

While sponsorship support from a corporation to a nonprofit is useful and greatly appreciated, it shouldn't be confused with philanthropy. True philanthropy is support of a cause without any commercial gain. Sponsorship is normally done more for promotion and advertising rather than solely for philanthropic reasons.

Be proactive about putting yourself and your cause out there to potential first-time business sponsors.

Sponsorship Tips

• Sometimes businesses like to be seen partnering with other businesses. They may see certain synergies to be gained through an alliance. Explore sponsorship opportunities that may align two or more businesses.

• Corporations like being associated with good will. Identify the services you provide that are most visible and accomplish the most good, then ask corporations to sponsor them.

One Event Sponsor or Many?

Don't overlook offering multiple sponsorship opportunities as ways to generate additional revenue and publicity.

Too many organizations — especially those organizing first-time fundraising events — make the mistake of assuming one event sponsor is sufficient. In addition to one major sponsor (or co-sponsors), why not break your event down into components that can be used to offer sponsorship opportunities for fewer dollars? Obviously, those sponsors putting up the most money will receive the greatest benefits and event visibility. However, sponsors underwriting smaller parts of your event can also receive benefits that will make the sponsorships worth their investments.

To help illustrate multiple sponsorship opportunities that your event may offer, examples of available sponsorships associated with a golfing event are listed below. You'll find it's easier to prioritize sponsor prospects and determine appropriate sponsor benefits by identifying sponsorship opportunities prior to approaching prospects.

Possible Sponsorship Opportunities Associated With a Golf Event

• Clinic sponsor	• Child care sponsor
• Registration sponsor	• Awards sponsor
• Hole sponsors	• Hole-in-one sponsor
• Tee sponsors	• Silent auction sponsor
• Valet parking sponsor	• Save-the-date and invitation sponsor
• Social hour sponsor	• Dinner sponsor
• Raffle sponsor	• Live auction sponsor

Develop a Process for Setting Prospect Appointments

Use an introductory letter to help set the stage for your appointment-setting call.

If your job includes making calls on would-be donors, it's important to religiously schedule appointments in advance.

To do so effectively, craft an introductory letter that you mail out one week prior to calling for the appointment. Your letter should grab the prospect's attention and set the stage for your appointment-setting call. The last sentence of your letter should emphasize that you will be calling within the next few days to schedule a visit.

Plan to send out at least one-third more letters each week than needed to fill your weekly schedule. For example, if you want to schedule 15 calls (on average) per week, send letters to 20 people, assuming not everyone will choose to meet with you.

By repeating this cycle, you will be able to establish a solid habit of appointment setting with new prospects.

GOAL: TO SCHEDULE 15 PROSPECT VISITS PER WEEK

Week 1	Week 2	Week 3
Send 20 prospect letters	Schedule appointments	Meet with 15 prospects

Raise $50,000 More in Sponsorships

Need an extra $50,000 in annual revenue? You can do it by building a set of action plans centered around one strategy. The key is picking a strategy best suited for your organization and sticking to it.

All too many nonprofits spread themselves too thin by doing a little more in direct mail, a little more in phonathons, a little more in face-to-face calls, etc. Instead, zero in on one fundraising strategy that makes sense for your organization and then build a set of sub-strategies around it.

Here are three examples of key strategy options broken down into sub-strategies that help illustrate this approach.

Three Focused Strategy Options to Generate $50,000 in New Gift Revenue

**Option No. 1: Longfellow Society (Annual Gifts of $1,000 or more)
Generate 50 New Members**

Member-recruit-a-member Initiative... Goal: $20,000
Staff Calls (Four new members per staff member)........................ Goal: $16,000
Targeted Direct Mail Appeal... Goal: $10,000
Board Development Committee.. Goal: $10,000

Option No. 2: New Sponsorships (To Underwrite Programs/Services)

Wellness Initiative..Goal: $20,000
Outreach/Mobile Unit...Goal: $10,000
Neo-natal...Goal: $20,000

Option No. 3: New Special Events

September Western-themed outdoor fundraiser.............................Goal: $15,000
December Tour of Homes..Goal: $18,000
April Fashion Show...Goal: $8,000
May Golf/Tennis Classic...Goal: $20,000

Enhance Sponsorship Revenue

Sponsorships — or lack of them — can be the difference between a prospering event and a floundering one. To augment this critical stream of revenue, Jean Block, president of Jean Block Consulting Inc. (Albuquerque, NM), advises event organizers to:

1. **Seek mission-matched sponsors**. In seeking sponsors, look for businesses that have a natural affinity for your mission, the people you serve, or the people who will attend your event. Less-traditional sponsors (e.g., businesses outside your immediate industry area) can be a significant source of untapped potential.

2. **Own the value of your event**. Your event is an important opportunity for sponsors to connect with potential customers, so own that value, says Block. "Businesses are often looking for more impact and visibility. Do some brainstorming, make a list of who would benefit from access to your events and attendees, and approach them with the opportunity to participate."

3. **Rethink sponsorship benefits**. Do your sponsors really care about the banner in the back of the room or the information table in the hallway? Block suggests asking long-time sponsors what benefits they would find most valuable.

4. **Over-deliver on promises**. Numerous nonprofits seek corporate support, so differentiate yourself from the pack by delivering the benefits you promised — and then some, says Block.

5. **Thank each sponsor at least three times**. The first gesture of appreciation should be a handwritten note as soon as a pledge is received. The second should warmly acknowledge the receipt of payment. The third should come after the event, and should enumerate the event's concrete results — dollars raised, programs funded, etc. — the donor's support made possible.

*Source: Jean Block, President, Jean Block Consulting Inc., Albuquerque, NM.
E-mail: jean@jblockinc.com.*

Securing sponsors for your nonprofit's first-ever event is just as important as securing sponsors for annual fundraisers. It sets the stage for attracting new businesses in the years to come.

SETTING THE SPONSORSHIP STAGE

For Sensitive Causes, Educate Before Soliciting Sponsorships

Lisa Smith, director, Sexual Assault and Crime Victims Assistance Program (Troy, NY), says her cause can be a tough sell when it comes to seeking sponsors.

"People have very distinct feelings about domestic violence. There's someone to blame. Some people even still blame the victim," Smith says. "In some cases, sponsors shy away from being aligned with potentially controversial causes like ours."

To overcome such situations and get potential sponsors and others to see the value of the organization, Smith uses education. "I don't set out to change people's minds, just open them a little," she says. "We don't want to be reactive. We want to be proactive and let them know (domestic violence) is not just a woman's issue."

Source: Lisa Smith, Director, Sexual Assault and Crime Victims Assistance Program, Samaritan Hospital, Troy, NY.. E-mail: smithlisa@nehealth.com

Have a relationship-buildling procedure in place to educate and nurture would-be sponsors before inviting them to invest in your cause.

'Scales of Giving' Aren't for Capital Campaigns Only

You're probably familiar with the "scale of giving" chart commonly used in conjunction with capital campaigns. The chart illustrates gift ranges for various gift amounts and identifies the number of donors needed in each category to achieve the campaign goal.

Although scales of giving appear to be less common with soliciting scholarships, they serve as a valuable tool in evaluating what will be required — number of sponsors, sponsorship levels, benefits — to meet your special event goal.

Develop a sponsorship scale-of-giving chart (like the sample chart below) that best reflects your organization's circumstances (e.g., constituency size, history of giving in various sponsorship ranges, fiscal year goal). You will find such a chart helpful in setting strategies for the year based on gifts required in each giving range.

As effective as "scales of giving" can be in helping meet gift goals for capital campaigns, they can also be useful in reaching sponsorship goals.

Sample scale of giving chart used to determine most appropriate fundraising strategies for the year.

SPONSORSHIP
SCALE OF GIVING CHART
2012/13 Goal: $700,000

Gift Range	No. of Gifts	Cumulative No. of Gifts	Number of Prospects	Cumulative No. of Prospects	Dollars/Range	Cumulative Dollars
$ 10,000	5	5	30 (6:1)	30	$50,000	$ 50,000
$ 5,000	10	15	50 (5:1)	80	$50,000	$ 100,000
$ 2,500	20	35	100 (5:1)	180	$50,000	$ 150,000
$ 1,000	50	85	200 (4:1)	380	$50,000	$ 200,000
		— 5 Percent of All Donors		60 Percent of Goal —		
$ 500	75	160	300 (4:1)	680	$37,500	$ 237,500
$ 250	100	260	300 (4:1)	980	$25,000	$ 262,500
$ 100	300	560	900 (4:1)	1880	$30,000	$ 292,500
		— 40 Percent of All Donors		27 Percent of Goal —		
Less than $100	700	1,260	1,400 (2:1)	3,280	$45,500	$ 338,000
		— 55 Percent of All Donors		13 Percent of Goal —		

Committees Should Have Yearly Goals and Objectives

Just as paid staff should have yearly goals and objectives — as identified in an operational plan — volunteers involved with securing sponsorships should also have a yearlong plan of action. Take the time to work with your sponsorship committee to identify quantifiable objectives that support goals and objectives. Rather than "informing" them of their responsibilities, engage them in a planning process that helps them more fully own those sponsorship-related objectives.

Once goals and objectives have been established for a committee, the written document should be monitored at regular meetings to measure progress being made throughout the year. Having such a plan of action for your sponsorship committee will help to keep them focused on achieving what matters most throughout the year.

Work with your sponsorship committee to establish a yearlong plan of goals and quantifiable objectives.

Use this template to develop a yearly plan of actions for your sponsorship committee.

XYZ CHARITY
2009 Fiscal Year
Goals and Objectives

COMMITTEE: Sponsorship Committee

GOAL
To assist the development department of XYZ Charity in achieving its annual goal of $100,000 in sponsorship revenue.

OBJECTIVES
1. To generate 25 new businesses/corporations ($1,000-and-above donors) by fiscal year end.

2. To net $30,000 by planning and executing the annual Golf Classic.

3. To coordinate and host five After Hours receptions aimed at area business professionals throughout the metro area.

Scheduled Meetings	Objective	Status	Next Steps	Scheduled Meetings	Objective	Status	Next Steps
July	1.			January	1.		
	2.				2.		
	3.				3.		
August	1.			February	1.		
	2.				2.		
	3.				3.		
September	1.			March	1.		
	2.				2.		
	3.				3.		
October	1.			April	1.		
	2.				2.		
	3.				3.		
November	1.			May	1.		
	2.				2.		
	3.				3.		
December	1.			June	1.		
	2.				2.		
	3.				3.		

IDENTIFYING SPONSORSHIP OPPORTUNITIES

Form Helps Avoid Seeking Sponsorships Haphazardly

Whether you want businesses to underwrite a special event, a new program you intend to launch or an existing budgeted project that can bring in additional revenue, your success will increase by doing some planning prior to approaching potential sponsors.

Make use of a "sponsorship project" form to help evaluate sponsorship opportunities and map out an action plan rather than haphazardly contacting prospects with little forethought. Here's a brief description of the form:

A. **Description of program/project** — Summarize the purpose of the program or project and what it entails.

B. **Anticipated start and duration of project/program** — When will the project begin? Will it be ongoing or is there an end date? Will the project/program be repeated? When and how often?

C. **Project/program components that could be underwritten** — Besides finding a major sponsor whose name might be associated with the event (e.g., The XYZ Golf Classic), are there parts within the project that could also be sponsored — a reception, training materials, exhibit area, etc.?

D. **Date, actions and person(s) responsible** — Outline anticipated steps that need to be taken in securing needed sponsorship support for the project/program and who is responsible for doing what by when.

E. **Project/program component, potential sponsors and solicitation target dates** — Identify and prioritize who might make the best sponsor candidates for each component of your project/program, and set deadlines for approaching them.

SPONSORSHIP PROJECT PLANNING FORM

Description of Program/Project _____

_____

Anticipated Start _____ Duration of Project/Program _____

Project/Program Components That Could Be Underwritten / **Sponsorship Cost**

1. _____ _____
2. _____ _____
3. _____ _____
4. _____ _____
5. _____ _____
6. _____ _____
7. _____ _____
8. _____ _____
9. _____ _____
10. _____ _____

Deadline	Actions	Person(s) Responsible

Project/Program Component	Potential Sponsors (Prioritized)	Solicitation Target Date

---

'Length of Time' Is a Key Sponsorship Variable

When approaching a business or corporation to sponsor a particular project, program or event, how much consideration do you give to the sponsorship's "duration?"

Granted, the time period for some sponsorship opportunities may be dictated by the project. A fundraising event, for instance, would be confined to the time prior to, during and immediately following the event. Some sponsorship opportunities may have more flexible timelines — the longer the timeline, the greater the sponsorship's cost.

As you examine various sponsorship opportunities, give thought to the period of time the project could be underwritten. Even a special event could have a multi-year time period if the sponsor was willing to lock into a multi-year agreement in return for extended publicity and visibility. Remember, the sponsorship timeline is a negotiable item.

The duration of each sponsorship opportunity will impact its dollar value.

Sponsorship Letter Reflects How Funds Will Benefit Others

To offer more opportunities for sponsors to support your special event, consider breaking down sponsorship levels by defining what those donated funds will do for the clients your organization serves.

HealthFinders (Northfield, MN) is a free clinic serving low-income residents in Rice County, MN. Operating two nights per week fully staffed requires significant funding to keep the doors open. An annual gala helps fund the organization's mission.

In 2009, HealthFinders staff created a sponsorship letter that not only lists the tangible benefits of sponsoring the gala, but more importantly, specifies how those sponsorship dollars would benefit clients of the clinic.

Here's how that information is communicated to potential sponsors:

Platinum Sponsor: $1,000

Sponsors at the $1,000 level receive recognition in the gala program, on HealthFinder's website, during the event and in the annual report, and are also given the following description of what the funds will do for the people who utilize the clinic:

> *"With your generous donation, HealthFinders will be able to provide 10 slots for the Pura Vida, weight management and nutrition program for six months and a month supply of medication to approximately 100 people."*

Gold Sponsor: $500

At the $500 level, sponsors receive the same recognitions as the platinum level, but more importantly, sponsors received information on how the sponsorship aids the clinic in the following tangible ways:

> *"With your generous donation, HealthFinders will be able to provide diabetic supplies to 10 diabetic patients for two months and two prescription chronic medications for two patients for one year."*

Silver Sponsor: $250

For a sponsorship of $250, the donor receives name recognition in the gala program and Healthfinder website as well as learning their funds will serve the following purpose:

> *"With your generous donation, HealthFinders will be able to provide diabetic supplies to 10 diabetic patients for one month or two prescription chronic medications for a patient for one year."*

Giving sponsors and potential sponsors a range of sponsorship levels, as well as details on how their support will benefit the cause, helps sell this important level of event support.

Source: Angelica Koch, Director, HealthFinders, Northfield, MN. Phone: (507) 330-4031. E-mail: koch.angelica@healthfindersmn.org. Website: www.healthfindersmn.org

Put Some Teeth Into Your Gift Club Through Sponsorships

Want to attract more $1,000-plus annual contributors? Maybe you need to bolster your top giving club to attract that level of giving.

Look to sponsors to underwrite particular costs that will help you identify, cultivate and steward donors at higher-end levels. Here are examples:

- Annual recognition banquet for $1,000-plus donors.
- Special thank-you mementos to recognize top donors
- A classy honor roll of contributors booklet that showcases your top gift club and lists those who gave at that level during the past fiscal year.
- Food, refreshments and entertainment for quarterly members-only receptions.
- Appropriate gratuities for upper-end donors.

If donors ever question how you can afford to provide so many perks for these more generous donors, you're able to point to the sponsors who underwrote those costs. Additionally, the sponsors know they are gaining visibility among your more affluent constituents.

Be prepared to offer a range of sponsorship opportunities that meet the interest level and ability of those you approach. In offering such sponsorship ranges however, be sure the accompanying benefits match the level of support. Top-level sponsorships should offer an exclusive range of benefits that make them far more compelling than lower-level sponsorships.

Here's a way for sponsors to actually help you raise more money: get them to sponsor costs associated with your top gift club.

IDENTIFYING SPONSORSHIP OPPORTUNITIES

Offer Businesses Varied Sponsorship Options

Regularly share and publicize a variety of sponsorship opportunities recognizing some will have greater appeal than others.

Wanting to broaden support from community and area businesses? Try offering different sponsorship options knowing some may be more appealing than others.

Whether you do it on a monthly or quarterly basis, develop a one- or two-page newsletter that includes varied sponsorship options each time it's sent out (or delivered) to businesses. In addition to the wish list of funding opportunities, your newsletter can include brief news items about your programs and services that may be of interest to businesses. Be sure to enclose a business reply envelope with each issue.

Sample page of a two-page newsletter distributed to businesses.

Creative Sponsor Names Reflect Event Themes

With a little bit of thought, you can come up with names for event sponsor levels that tie your event together by reflecting your theme and reminding people why they're there.

Here are two examples of unique names, used by officials at Circle of Friends (Austin, TX) to help make their events gel:

- For their Angels on Wheels Motorcycle Ride, all sponsor level names reflect the heavenly theme, including heavenly angel ($25,000), archangel ($10,000), guardian angel ($5,000), angel ($2,500) and cherub ($250).

- For their American Girl Fashion Show, sponsor level names reflect things that little girls dream about, including diamond ($10,000), glitter ($5,000), stardust ($2,500), sparkle ($1,000) and tea party ($500).

Source: Jayme Clark, Circle of Friends Coordinator, Dell Children's Medical Center, Austin, TX.
E-mail: jsclark@seton.org

News for Area Businesses from ABC Nonprofit

Many thanks to the following businesses who contributed to last quarter's Support a Child effort:

- Acme Printing
- Beleme Brothers
- Dance Away
- Ely Manufacturing
- Tools & Tools
- Wheterhoos Services

ABC Nonprofit helped serve 544 under-privileged youth during the last quarter. Our efforts are helping enrich the lives of area youth who will one day be contributing members of this community and region.

Thanks to these businesses that donated in-kind services last quarter:

Bell's Printing	El Fredo Pizza
Heartland, Inc.	Tri-state Steel

2nd Quarter Funding Opportunities

We invite area businesses to help sponsor all or part of the Fall Field Trip for Youth. Some of the sponsorship opportunities associated with this annual field trip include:

Overall sponsor	$10,000
Transportation	$2,500
Attraction and educational fees	$2,000
Food	$200/child
Lodging	$100/child
Supervision	$50/child

See Page 2 for Sponsorship Benefits! Return the enclosed envelope to make your gift or learn more.

The Fall Field Trip allows up to 200 disadvantaged youth to participate in a three-day field trip that's both fun-filled and educational. Participants will visit a museum, a manufacturing facility, the State Capitol, a nature preserve and spend time meeting with mentors who will share their life experiences with these deserving young people. In addition, the children will spend an afternoon at the Whittleon Water Park. This will be the only travel most of these youth will have ever experienced.

Did you know? — ABC Nonprofit has an annual payroll of $754,000, contributing to the overall economic vitality of our community.

Mark your calendar — Plan to attend the ABC Nonprofit open house scheduled to take place on September 14 from 4 to 7 pm. Meet your community's youth and see the newly renovated Learning Center.

Get Sponsors to Underwrite Publications Costs

Looking for ways to cut back on expenses and raise more money at the same time? Get businesses and/or individuals to underwrite every one of your nonprofit's publications.

Begin by developing a menu that lists each of your nonprofit's publications along with sponsorship prices and brief descriptions of each. (See generic example)

You may wish to list sponsor benefits associated with each publication or address those perks as you meet with would-be donors. Minimally, each publication would say "This publication made possible through the generosity of..."

You may choose to begin with a limited number of publication sponsorship opportunities and then keep expanding your list in subsequent years.

This method of raising gifts will be more attractive to many than simply asking for an outright gift that supports general operations. Donors can see exactly how their gifts are being used to help your nonprofit.

Offer businesses, even individuals, the opportunity to underwrite the cost of every printed piece you produce.

This partial list of publiciation sponsorship opportunities illustrates how you might create a menu suited to your nonprofit's publications.

XYZ Hospital Foundation

Publication Sponsorship Opportunities

To help direct more of the hospital's limited resources toward valuable patient services, we invite you to underwrite one or more of our hospital's regularly printed publications. Each sponsorship opportunity carries with it certain
benefits which will be shared with interested parties:

❑ **Annual Giving Brochure (Yearly)**   **Cost: $900**

This publication serves as the Development Office's primary tool for inviting gift annual support. Sponsorship of this publication helps the hospital foundation broaden its base of annual support.

❑ **Planned Giving Newsletter (Quarterly)**   **Cost: $1,800**

This valuable resource helps to nurture planned gifts (bequests, annuities and more) that will ensure our hospital's future. In the past year alone, the hospital received $650,000 in bequests.

❑ **Heartbeat Magazine Annual Report (Yearly)**   **Cost: $4,000**

This annual "report card" addresses the hospital's key challenges and accomplishments and is intended to give you a clear and concise picture of your hospital. It also lists those who have generously contributed to the hospital's foundation during the past year.

❑ **Heartbeat Magazine (Three Times Per Year)** **Cost: $9,000**

This award-winning magazine is distributed to everyone on our mailing list (former patients, clients, community leaders, area businesses and more).

❑ **Preventative Publications (Yearly)**   **Cost: Varies**

Each year (every two years in some instances), the hospital publishes handouts that help to educate the public on various wellness issues (diet, nutrition, exercise and more). These resources are invaluable in helping our citizenry maintain and improve good health practices.

Boost Sponsorship Revenue

To increase the number of sponsors for your organization and increase existing sponsors' level of support, create a ladder of sponsorship opportunities.

Develop a list of all available sponsorship opportunities arranged in least- to most-expensive order. Each increasing level should obviously include more attractive benefits for the would-be sponsor.

When calling on new prospects, offer less-costly sponsorship opportunities to get them on board with your organization. Invite those with a history of sponsorships to a higher level with more exclusive benefits.

This laddering method will help you add new sponsors and move existing sponsors toward increased levels of support.

When Leveraging Naming Opportunities, Consistency is Key

Naming opportunities provide one of the most dependable sources of revenue for advanced institutions and other nonprofits, particular in construction projects and capital campaigns. But the sale of naming rights — equal parts art and science — is not as simple or straightforward as it might seem.

Bobby Couch, executive director of major gifts for Clemson University Athletics (Clemson, SC), shares valuable insights on this important type of fundraising.

Philosophically, how should organizations approach the sale of naming rights?

"In my opinion, many organizations are too quid-pro-quo, and the sale of naming rights becomes almost like selling a piece of real estate. At Clemson, we try to make naming opportunities more a part of donor stewardship, more of a way for donors to feel close and connected to the institution they are supporting."

On what should a naming rights policy focus?

"Consistency and equivalency. You want to make sure that X amount of donation receives X amount of recognition, regardless of the donor or the program donated to. So our policy [shown right] clearly defines the size of plaque, the size of lettering, the font used to recognize different levels of gift. That way everything is consistent, and we can have samples to show potential donors exactly what their recognition would look like."

Does consistency mean premium naming opportunities should be avoided?

"No. Donors understand that you will take the prestige of a program into consideration when pricing its facilities. If your men's tennis team regularly wins major tournaments or your fine arts program is ranked in the top ten nationwide, the right to name its elements will naturally command a higher price."

Are expiration clauses on naming opportunities appropriate?

"There is somewhat of an industry trend in that direction, particularly with corporate donors. With the frequency of mergers and acquisitions, corporate names that make sense today can be obsolete within a few years. For that reason, we tend to limit our corporate naming to five- and ten-year terms. We also revisit corporate naming more frequently and use more contractual agreements with corporate donors."

How is the sale of naming rights different with regard to facilities under construction?

"There are two rules of thumb with new construction. The first is that naming rights for the entire facility should be priced at 25 percent of construction costs or more. The price to name the new $10 million swimming center, for example, should not be less than $2.5 million. Second, you want all your other naming rights to generate more revenue than construction costs, ideally up to around 150 percent. So you would want all the rest of the naming opportunities for the center to produce around $12.5 million. Those two rules provide the structure for pricing all your individual naming opportunities."

What about 'morality clauses' or guidelines?

"The advancement staff at Clemson have pretty wide latitude for any gifts under $1 million. For anything over that, there is a named gifts committee that goes through a very thorough due diligence and considers any issues that might reflect poorly on the institution. The committee can also revisit the naming if an incident occurs with the donor at a later date."

What is the biggest mistake you see in selling naming rights?

"The tendency to under price. Most naming rights are for perpetuity, but hopefully your institution will grow and its programs will become more popular. Because of these changes, it's important to price on the high end, rather than the low end."

Source: Bobby Couch, Executive Director of Major Gifts, Clemson University Athletics/IPTAY, Clemson, SC. Phone (864) 656-0361. E-mail: Jcouch@clemson.edu

---

Steps Help Determine Prices For Naming Opportunities

How should an organization go about pricing naming opportunities? By following four specific steps, says Bobby Couch, executive director of major gifts for Clemson University Athletics (Clemson, SC).

Couch shares those steps:

1. First, go through your facilities and make an inventory — all the rooms, offices, lockers, fields, etc.
2. Next, categorize the inventory — what is high or low visibility, what is in public traffic ways, what will be named in perpetuity and what might be moved/repurposed in the future.
3. As you begin pricing things, research what your peer institutions are charging for naming similar assets.
4. Finally, make sure that your prices are consistent with each other and that comparable opportunities have comparable prices.

Couch shares guidelines that help guarantee consistency of donor recognition for Clemson University's West Zone Initiative fundraising campaign:

- **$10,000 – 49,999**: Standard signage similar to directional signage materials but still distinguishing in appearance
- **$50,000 – 149,999**: 10X12 plaques only
- **$150,000 – 249,999**: 12X14 plaques & aluminum/bronze lettering (4 in.)
- **$250,000 – 999,999**: up to 16X16 plaques & aluminum/bronze lettering (greater than 5 in.)
- **$1 million**: 20X20 plaques w/image casting, aluminum/bronze lettering (greater than 5 in.) along with Bronze Lettering on inside façade of WZone Complex
- **> or = $5 million**: Name to appear at pinnacle of inside façade of WZone Complex as well as front entrance

Create Profiles of Would-be Sponsors

What are you doing to maximize success when it comes to soliciting support from the business community? Whether you use a particular prospect management software or a form such as the example below, your time and ultimate success will be best used by planning and prioritizing anticipated calls on businesses.

The process of learning who the key players are, discovering a business' recent history of giving, determining any existing links to your organization and more will increase your odds for success as you map out a plan of research, cultivation and solicitation.

You might even consider forming a business advisory council made up of volunteers familiar with your business community to review names of — and make calls — on businesses capable of making generous gifts. A form similar to this would be helpful in providing ongoing direction to your most capable volunteers.

Mapping out a plan to approach business prospects will be helpful in your solicitation efforts.

Why not form a business advisory council to identify likely sponsors and make calls on them?

BUSINESS PROSPECT PROFILE & ANTICIPATED MOVES SCHEDULE

Name of Business _____

Address _____

City _____ State _____ Zip _____

Key Company Contacts	Titles	Phone Numbers

Known Philanthropic Recipients	Appr. Date	Gift/Sponsor Use

Matching gift company?　☐ Yes　☐ No
Published gift/grant guidelines?　☐ Yes　☐ No
Formal gifts committee/process?　☐ Yes　☐ No

Links to our organization:
1. _____　3. _____
2. _____　4. _____

Likely gift/sponsorship opportunities based on what we know today:
1. _____　3. _____
2. _____　4. _____

Anticipated plan for introduction:

Who	When	Objective

Anticipated cultivation moves:

When	What	By Whom

Target Amount: $ _____

Anticipated solicitation:

When	Gift Use	By Whom

IDENTIFYING & PRIORITIZING LIKELY SPONSORS

Grid System Prioritizes Funding Sources

Use a grid to help identify and prioritize your sponsorship opportunities before asking businesses to support your cause.

The process of narrowing down and prioritizing funding sources provides much greater focus in identifying and pursuing corporation and business sponsors. This prospect prioritization grid can be a useful tool to help you in this important process.

1. To begin, it's important to know your organization's needs and develop a sense of funding priorities. **For instance, is library renovation more important than new science labs?** The ability to categorize needs will help to know which projects to pursue most rigorously. You may want to form a sponsorship committee to collectively prioritize funding needs. Those projects receiving "A" ratings, for instance, are of highest priority, while those with "C" ratings are desirable, but least important.

2. Once you identify your funding needs, initiate an ongoing commitment to review publications and periodicals publicizing sponsorship opportunities.

3. After reviewing publications best addressing your interests, list the businesses or corporations that may be most interested in underwriting your event/project.

4. If available, include the names of one or two organizations that received funding in case you choose to contact them for further information.

5. Finally, check those categories matching the business or corporation that would be most appropriate to meet your organization's needs.

This grid format helps focus funding efforts on businesses and corporations most closely related to your organization's specific needs and programs.

Content not available in this edition

Create a Corporate Identity

Win potential sponsors' attention and respect by being an active member of the corporate community.

What goes around comes around. That's why, at least among area businesses, your organization should be perceived as a member of the local corporate/business community. While yours may be a not-for-profit entity, those in business are more easily sold on your cause if they recognize your economic impact. This is especially important as you look toward businesses within your community to underwrite an event/project.

What can you do to be more fully perceived as a corporate member of the community? Use this checklist to determine what additional steps to take:

❏ Become an active member of the local chamber of commerce.
❏ Be attuned to local issues and ways in which your organization might respond to community needs that are in line with your mission.
❏ Spell out ways in which your organization positively impacts the local or area economy — number of employees, total payroll, how your presence saves taxpayers and more.
❏ Conduct business locally to the degree possible.
❏ Be alert to opportunities in which your facilities and/or services might be more fully opened to and utilized by the community.

Tap Into Corporate Marketing Budgets to Increase Funds

Typically, nonprofits focus on tapping into a company's philanthropic budget, but unfortunately, in today's corporate business environment, those philanthropic budgets are shrinking, says Jean Block, of Jean Block Consulting, Inc. (Albuquerque, NM).

"It's not likely that corporate philanthropic budgets will increase any significant amount in the coming years," she says. "Although philanthropic money is still there, that is charitable money that comes to you because there is a heart connection and a mission connection."

Corporate advertising, marketing and business development budgets, however, are not shrinking, says Block, and in many cases they are growing because businesses are in a more competitive environment than ever before.

"How you tap into a company's advertising, marketing and business development budgets is very different than how you tap into their philanthropic budget," she says. "It's not as much about mission as it's about how you can help the company meet their business marketing needs, and promote their business to your market."

That means that when it comes to developing a sponsorship proposal, one size does not fit all, says Block.

It's also important to differentiate between different programs and events, says Block.

Source: Jean Block, Jean Block Consulting, Inc., Albuquerque NM. E-mail: jean@jblockinc.com

---

Convert Advertisers Into Sponsors

Who should you consider as possible sponsors for an event or program? Start with businesses that are currently doing a lot of advertising. Begin tracking:

- ✓ Where they are advertising, and how often.
- ✓ The audience you believe they are trying to reach.
- ✓ What their ads are saying.

By monitoring companies' advertising, you can begin to make assumptions of whether particular companies may make good sponsorship prospects. Use what you learn to make your case about why a sponsorship with your organization makes sense.

Know Who's Getting Your Business

Did your charity recently make a big purchase? Which local realtors benefited from having your new employees as clients? Have any employee groups sponsored a dinner or reception at a local restaurant?

While a charity's selection of business vendors should generally not take past contributions into consideration, the reverse can be helpful in the solicitation process. Knowing which businesses are benefitting from your organization and its employees (and how much) can help in the timing of a solicitation, the ask amount and even the type of gift you may choose to solicit (e.g., cash or gift-in-kind).

Invite your organization's business office and employees to help you track where and when they are doing official business. Distribute a business activity form to all employees, encouraging them to complete and return it to you each time they conduct official business.

As easy as it may be for you to periodically receive a vendor report from your business office, this more comprehensive method may pinpoint purchases/expenditures that the business office alone is unable to produce. And, it's not only the amount of the expenditure that matters; your charity's prominence in the eyes of a business may have equal or greater impact.

LANCASTER ART CENTER — Business Activity Form

Please complete and return this form each time you or a group of employees conducts official business in our community/region. Your willingness to keep us updated may prove valuable as we cultivate and solicit gift support. Thank you for your valuable assistance.

Employee/Department Submitting Form: _____
Date Submitted: _____
Name of Business Benefitting from LAC: _____
Business Contact: _____
Approximate Amount of Purchase/Expenditure: _____
    Date of Purchase/Expenditure: _____
    Type of Purchase/Expenditure: _____
Number of LAC employees involved: _____
Is this a recurring purchase/expenditure? ❑ Yes   ❑ No
    If so, when and how often? _____
How/why did you select this business? _____
Were you satisfied with the purchase/expenditure? *(Please describe)*
_____

Would you make a similar purchase/expenditure with this business again? Why or why not? _____
_____

Additional comments that might provide insight into the cultivation/solicitation of this prospect: _____
_____

IDENTIFYING & PRIORITIZING LIKELY SPONSORS

Compare Similar Vendors' Giving History

A look at your organization's vendors' giving history can give you an idea of who might be viable sponsorship prospects.

It's wise, from time to time, to review your organization's list of vendors to determine who is giving and who is not. It can also be useful to compare your organization's relationship with similar, perhaps competing, companies, evaluating the amount of business you give each with their level of giving to your organization. A closer review may point out that one company which gives modestly is getting the bulk of your organization's business while a competing company giving at a much higher level is receiving much less of your purchasing dollars.

While many nonprofit executives will argue that purchasing decisions should be made separately from if or how much a business chooses to contribute, there's no doubt that a vendor should be considered a viable gift prospect. And while other factors may have higher priority in your nonprofit's business decisions (e.g., price, quality of workmanship, etc.), level of gift support should at least be given some consideration.

To better evaluate similar and/or competing vendors, consider making use of a report similar to the one below on a quarterly basis.

Review and compare similar vendors' business activity and level of giving.

QUARTERLY VENDOR REVIEW

For Period Ending _____   Distribute To _____

Vendor	Item/Description	Date	Amount	Gift History			
				01/09	02/10	03/11	Current
Print Vendors							
1. ABC Printing	Gala programs	8/5/11	$1,200	$50	$50	$50	$100
2. Blue Ink Print & Design	Invitations	8/15/11	$1,744	$500	$700	$800	$1,000
Real Estate Vendors							
1. Century 21/Bill Tompson	Silver Sponsor	7/6/11	$7,000	—	$30	—	—
2. Nodlund Realty/Sue Nodlund	Golf Classic Tee Sponsor	7/10/11	$1,200	$400	$400	$400	$500
Soft Drink Vendors							
1. Semple Coca Cola Distributors	Soft drinks	8/1/11	$3,123	$2,000	$2,000	$2,000	$2,000
2. Hilman Pepsi Distributor Co.	Soft drinks	8/3/11	$1,214	$900	$1,000	$1,000	$1,250

Secure Sponsors to Underwrite Your Appeals

Ask Vendors To Help Make Introductions

In addition to financial contributions, your organization's vendors can be a great source of help introducing you to other business contacts — if you ask for their help.

Meet with vendors individually and ask them to come up with a list of those individuals and organizations with whom they do business. Then review the list together to determine those to whom they would be willing to introduce you.

Do you have multiple direct mail appeals throughout the year? Why not ask businesses or individuals to sponsor individual appeals or your entire annual package of mailings?

By encouraging a business or individual(s) to sponsor an appeal — underwriting its total cost with a gift — you can accomplish several objectives:

• The sponsoring donor sees exactly how his/her gift is used — in this case, to generate more money for the organization.

• The sponsor gains new visibility: "This mailing underwritten by..."

• You save needed budget dollars for other worthwhile programs.

• You gain greater financial flexibility in creating an attention-getting appeal.

Build Business Alliances

As you work to build relationships with businesses, exhaust every opportunity to forge alliances with employees who work for those companies. They may be helpful at influencing their company's top decision makers.

To network with as many company employees as possible:

1. Don't miss an opportunity to make a presentation or offer a facilities tour to a group of company employees.

2. Explore the feasibility of having news of your organization and its work placed in the company's newsletter.

3. Meet with those company employees who are already committed to your cause and form an ambassador committee, charging them to help speak on your behalf to colleagues.

Don't Overlook Regional, National Companies

There are many foundations and companies that have an online application process for sponsorships, grants and funds. All of them have guidelines as to who can or can't receive funds and what procedures must be followed.

Here are some examples of regional or national companies that consider sponsorships:

C&S Wholesale Grocers — www.cswg.com/community/sponsor.htm

Gannett Foundation — www.gannettfoundation.org

Gap, Inc — www.gapinc.com (Click on Social Responsibility, select Community Involvement, then Giving Money.)

Sara Lee for Youth Foundation — www.saraleefoundation.org

Make Connections Through Businesses' Vendors

That tried-and-tested saying of "people don't give to organizations, people give to people," is just as true of the business community as it is of individuals.

When it comes to garnering new business and corporate support, it makes a great deal of sense to scrutinize the links existing supporters have with other businesses. Some of your donors may hold board positions; others will no doubt carry on vendor relationships with many businesses.

That's why it is worth the time to compile and maintain vendor lists for your existing business donors. With whom do each of them do business? Once you have lists in place for each supporting business, you can begin to explore those relationships and determine which, among them, hold the greatest potential of making generous gifts to your organization.

In prioritizing business' vendors as gift prospects, it's important to gauge the willingness and ability of each existing donor to help introduce your agency and assist in the solicitation process. Ask yourself in each case, "How much business does this donor do with this company? Is it considered a big account?"

You may even choose to develop some form of rating scale to help measure the potential of each based on factors including: willingness/ability of the donor to assist in solicitation, importance of this donor's business to the vendor prospect, financial ability of vendor prospect, etc.

Remember to look for both obvious and not-so-obvious vendor relationships as you build each list.

Obvious Examples of Businesses' Vendors

Donor	Donor's Vendors
Bread manufacturer	Distributor of flour
Automobile dealer	Newspapers, radio and television stations (advertising)
Printing company	Paper distributors Printing equipment distributors
Furniture store	Furniture distributors Carpet distributors Wall-covering distributors

Three Tips for Seeking Corporate Sponsorship

The Monmouth County Society for the Prevention of Cruelty to Animals (Eatontown, NJ), has just begun seeking the assistance of corporate sponsors to support its mission of protecting animals.

A feel-good community event with common goal helps establish strong relationships with corporate/busienss donors, resulting in added sponsorship revenue.

Stephanie Attaway, development coordinator, and Lisa Mulhearn, communications professional, share some of the lessons they have learned in this process:

1. Approach businesses with an existing relationship with your nonprofit such as your bank, phone service provider, utility company, etc. The potential in this group is vast.
2. Look for companies that have a strong reputation for community support. Seek the advice from your local chamber of commerce to determine philanthropic corporations in your area.
3. Find companies that have foundations or matching funds programs that could benefit your mission.

Source: Stephanie Attaway, Development Coordinator, and Lisa Mulhearn, Communications Professional, Monmouth County Society for the Prevention of Cruelty to Animals, Eatontown, NJ. E-mail: stephanie@monmouthcountyspca.org.

Create Extended Family Sponsorship Opportunities

Families today are volunteering together; why not ask them to donate together?

Look to extended families to sponsor particular programs or events.

Ask members of an extended family (by starting with one or two related donors or prospects in your database) to pool their resources to fund a specific project or program they can all get behind with their support.

Not only is this a great way to expand your donor base, a unique sponsorship such as this could attract positive attention of the news media. Think of it: "The 23-member Poole family together donated $15,000 to fund our organization's community outreach program."

The media attention just may attract additional families interested in creating their own extended family partnerships.

Personalized Mailing Finds New Sponsors

While securing generous sponsorships requires one-on-one visits, direct mail can help to surface interested prospects.

Craft a personalized letter (and maybe a program or event summary sheet) to send to a large number of potential sponsors. Summarize sponsorship opportunities and point out the direct benefits of being a sponsor (publicity, free tickets, targeted exposure, etc.).

Include a "bounce back" form (see example at left) and return envelope inviting potential sponsors to express interest in learning more about sponsorship opportunities.

By directing a personalized mailing to a larger number of possible sponsors, you can attempt to surface those who have an interest in exploring sponsorships. This allows you to prioritize calls and avoids spinning your wheels contacting businesses and individuals with no interest in exploring sponsorship opportunities.

Sponsorship Opportunities at XYZ Agency

Return this form to learn more about sponsorship opportunities and the benefits you can receive by becoming a sponsor. We'll contact you to set up a no-obligation, confidential appointment.

_____ Yes, I'd like to explore sponsorship opportunities.

_____ I'm particularly interested in the following sponsorship possibilities mentioned in your letter:

1. _____
2. _____
3. _____

Name _____ Title _____

Organization _____

Daytime Phone _____ E-mail _____

Sample bounce back used with letter to would-be sponsors.

Provide Event Sponsors With Invitations to Distribute

If your corporate sponsorship includes allowing the company to bring guests to your events for their support, consider sending them invitations they can use.

One nonprofit in Princeton, NJ made it easy for sponsors to invite guests by offering free tickets to the chapter's annual Polo Classic as a benefit to its varying levels of sponsorship.

Here's how it works: If a sponsor is entitled to bring 150 guests, the nonprofit sends 150 invitations to the corporate contact at the company. They then send those invitations to whomever they choose. Not only is this benefit convenient for the sponsor but it also offers added benefits to the nonprofit.

Play Up Your Most Appealing Sponsorship Perks

Here are some sponsorship benefits nonprofits are offering their corporate sponsors:

Make the sponsorship exclusive. Aspen Music Festival and School (Aspen, CO) promises that its corporate sponsors won't get lost in a "sea of logos." One of the organization's sponsorship benefits is exclusivity by offering targeted sponsorship opportunities that provide maximum exposure for the lead sponsor(s).

Name drop. At the Columbus Museum of Art (Columbus, OH) $50,000-plus corporate sponsors get their names mentioned on the museum's 24-hour information line, which tells callers about the current exhibitions, programs and events at the museum.

Look for unique sponsorship benefits tailored to each business you approach.

Exposures count. The Preservation Society of Newport County, aka The Newport Mansions (Newport, RI), offers its corporate sponsors visibility. The museum boasts more than 500,000 visitors each year. Corporate sponsors get their corporate name and logo on 1 million preservation society brochures and admission tickets, and on the organization's website, which averages 1 million hits per year.

Attention to employees. Minuteman Senior Services (Burlington, MA) offers its corporate sponsors on-site seminars for their employees on elder caregiver issues.

Recognize 'What's In It' for the Corporate Donor

Corporate prospect research is about more than knowing how much money a corporation is able or willing to give. It's also about knowing what the corporation will get out of making a gift. So when researching a corporate prospect, remember to factor in "what's in it for them?" This information will also help you in developing your solicitation approach. Use this checklist:

✓ Are their consumers your donors or alumni?

✓ Do they recruit on your campus?

✓ Have they sponsored research contracts or grants?

✓ Have they sponsored similar events for similar organizations?

✓ Do they serve on your board or the boards of similar organizations?

✓ Does their corporate volunteer and/or donation program fit with your mission?

Always Remember: WIIFM?

Whether meeting with a would-be donor face-to-face, making an ask through a direct mail or online appeal or soliciting a gift by phone, always keep the WIIFM — What's In It For Me? — factor in mind.

Every request for support should address donor benefits.

SELECTING APPROPRIATE SPONSORSHIP PERKS

Attract Corporate Sponsors by Providing Ample Perks

Corporate sponsorships distribute thousands of dollars each year in support of nonprofit goals. To draw significant corporate sponsorship, offer the following perks to attract corporate sponsorships:

- Create a Support our Sponsors section of your newsletter.
- Add an endorsement section to your website that prominently features your corporate sponsors and the product or service they provide.
- Create a wall of appreciation within your nonprofit featuring plaques or labels naming your corporate sponsors.
- Prepare framed certificates or plaques that you can present to your corporate sponsors which they can hang in their place of business. This gift is a win-win, as your nonprofit will receive more notoriety and the corporate sponsor will receive deserved kudos for their gifts.
- Feature corporate sponsor logos in your lobby to immediately acknowledge your corporate sponsors.

It is important to distinguish the difference between donor benefits and sponsor benefits prior to approaching businesses/corporations.

Leverage Green Credentials To Boost Fundraising Efforts

Is your institution cutting energy use, growing its own food or building environmentally friendly facilities? Use those green credentials to advance major fundraising efforts.

Rob White, director of alumni communications at Williams College (Williamstown, MA), shares ways environmental practices can aid advancement efforts:

✓ **Support of sustainability itself**. "When our board of trustees decided to meet the Kyoto protocol environmental standards by 2020, one alumnus indicated his interest in helping realize that commitment. Previously he had not been particularly engaged with Williams, but those conversations resulted in a $5 million gift that helped create a new center for sustainability and environmental initiatives."

✓ **Young alumni engagement**. "Moving the majority of annual solicitations to e-mail has been huge for our younger alumni. More and more were starting to say, 'If you don't stop killing trees to ask me for money, I'm not going to give you anything.'"

✓ **Larger capital gifts**. "We've been able to command somewhat larger gifts for our two building projects that were LEED (Leadership in Energy and Environmental Design) Gold certified. That certification was a large part of the buildings' appeal to major donors."

✓ **Donor attraction and retention**. Sound environmental practices are as much about projecting an image of leadership as prompting specific gifts, says White. "If we are not substantially and visibly in the forefront of the sustainability movement, we can assume that a growing proportion of the philanthropy we would have received will be directed somewhere else."

While green initiatives vary widely in emphasis and focus, White says donors generally prefer programs that directly support people and communities. At Williams, a community garden program is popular and a sustainable food and agriculture program recently received funding, while new programs of study in sustainability and environmental studies are garnering support.

Source: Rob White, Director of Alumni Communications, Williams College, Williamstown, MA. E-mail: rwhite@williams.edu

Seven Unique Benefits to Offer Event Sponsors

The logo on the event program. The banner on the website. The complementary set of VIP tickets. You know the kinds of benefits businesses are always offered in return for sponsorship support — and chances are they do too.

There's nothing with these tried-and-true perks, but offering a few new twists might make your event stand out to potential sponsors. Consider the following for a few new ideas:

- **Event status designations.** Your event has moral and/or professional weight. Use that influence by offering potential sponsors the opportunity to earn a "preferred supplier status", or to give one of their products an official product status (e.g. official running shoe of a marathon, official wireless provider of a conference.)
- **On-site display opportunities.** Your event will be bringing together a large number of people around a narrow theme. This can be a golden opportunity for the right businesses. Let them conduct on-site sampling, demonstrations and/or displays in return for generous sponsorship support.
- **Access to "talent."** Celebrities will attract participants to your event participants, but they will also be a draw for sponsors. Offer access to your well-known headliners, whether through private meetings or exclusive events held with key staff or clients, as part of your benefit package.
- **Database marketing.** The database generated by your event's registration process might be of great interest to potential sponsors. Consider giving access to it for a company's direct mail initiatives, but be sure to offer this benefit only sparingly. You don't want to drive people away from your event with a flood of unsolicited mail.
- **Employment recruiting.** Businesses are always looking for the best and the brightest, and your event might be just the place to find them. Give select sponsors the opportunity to set up a staff recruitment display and/or distribute recruitment information.
- **Proof of purchase promotion.** Looking to woo retail-oriented sponsors? Help drive business their way by discounting admission, parking or merchandise at your event with proof of purchase from their stores.
- **Charitable support.** Businesses look at the bottom line, but that's not always the only thing they look at. Socially conscious companies might be attracted by an offer to involve the sponsor's chosen charity in the event or donate a small portion of ticket sales to it.

Give each guests a goodie bag as they depart that includes product or services information from each of your sponsors, both guests and sponsors will appreciate it.

Table Tents Extend Event Sponsors' Placement

The Hermann London Halloween 5K, a charity run organized by the Hermann London Group (Maplewood, MO) a for-profit real estate company for the benefit of a local women's shelter and the Missouri Coalition Against Domestic and Sexual Violence, uses table tents at restaurants as a unique way to lure race sponsors to its cause.

Hermann London Founder Adam Kruse describes the table tents as "an innovative way of helping the sponsors get value out of sponsoring us other than on race day." While race sponsors do receive more common promotional placements as well — such as their logos on race T-shirts and collateral materials inside runners' gift bags — table tents at local restaurants offer sponsors the opportunity to see their association with the race extended to those other than race-day participants, and for much longer than one day.

Kruse says that race organizers stick to "sports bar types of places" when determining which restaurants they should ask to display the table tents. As a simple and time-saving strategy to reach as many such restaurants as possible, Kruse worked through a local liquor representative who distributed the table tents to his area clients on Hermann London's behalf.

"It prolonged our message, spread awareness and got more racers to the event," Kruse says — all benefits to the race itself, while offering sponsors prime placement for local advertising.

To make event's sponsors feel even more special, arrange to have them picked up and dropped off at your event in a limousine.

Source: Adam Kruse, Founder, The Hermann London Group, Maplewood, MO.
E-mail: adam@hermannlondonl.com.

Goals Help Prioritize Funding Needs

Those responsible for developing sponsorship proposals at your institution can benefit from having a one-year (or multi-year) operational plan that prioritizes not only funding needs, but also quantifies deadlines and target amounts.

As you map out quantifiable funding objectives for one year or more, categorize them within the following groups: program goals, equipment goals, project goals and event goals.

A simple chart like the example shown here helps to prioritize funding needs and, as a result, top sponsorship goals.

		For What	By When	For How Much
Program Goals:	1.			
	2.			
	3.			
Equipment Goals:	1.			
	2.			
	3.			
Project Goals:	1.			
	2.			
	3.			
Event Goals:	1.			
	2.			
	3.			

Tips for Writing Winning Proposals

Are you emphasizing "opportunities" or "needs" as you write your sponsorship proposal? Do you include copies of testimonials from satisfied clientel in the appendices of your proposal? Is it alright to use photos and graphics to illustrate points throughout a proposal?

Here are several tips to consider in developing winning sponsorship proposals:

- Review your proposal draft with a critical eye. Ask yourself what the strongest objections might be and then counter them.

- Demonstrate that you're serious about your request by illustrating the kinds of follow-up and activities that will take place once the funds have been received.

- Write your cover letter in such a way that, if the proposal were lost, the business would have a clear understanding of what is being requested and for what purpose.

- Be confident in your approach to businesses. Don't be apologetic. Be forceful without being pushy.

- Know as much as possible about your prospect before starting to write your proposal.

- Get your project/event critiqued by a number of associates before writing a full-scale proposal.

- Don't try for perfection on your first draft — get down your ideas, then edit and rewrite.

- Have a strong first sentence and a strong ending.

- Write your budget first. Make sure your proposal supports each item in that budget.

- Begin your proposal with the most important point — don't make it a mystery.

- If appropriate, quote the businesses' annual report to show how your project fits their goals.

Make Proposals Digestible

Whether in print publications, direct-mail pieces or on your website, writing should not just be clear and understandable — it should appear easy to read in terms of type size, font and spacing.

A full page of single-spaced type will intimidate even the most avid reader.

To make your writing appear less formidable, break up the page into small paragraphs with subheads. Allowing the reader to digest smaller portions of information at a time will make your writing much more readable. This, in turn, will help guarantee your carefully chosen words reach — and move — your audiences as you intended.

Event Sponsor Proposals Need Not be Complicated

Most successful events today owe a big part of that success to sponsorships.

Whether you're organizing a fundraiser or other type of event, sponsorships not only cover the costs associated with an event, they can generate profit as well.

Sharing a written proposal with would-be sponsors is a crucial first step to securing support. Depending on the amount you seek, a proposal needn't be all that lengthy or complicated. In fact, some would-be sponsors prefer a simple one-page proposal that gets right to the point.

Although there is no particular format for drafting a sponsorship proposal, here is one format you can use as a guide in developing one that best fits your organization and proposed event. This example includes the following components:

Sponsorship proposals help turn a plan of action into results.

- **Event summary** — The summary should briefly describe the event: its purpose, why you need one or more sponsors and the benefits to the sponsor(s).

- **Introduction** — Include a brief description of your organization and how this event will help to address your mission.

- **Event description** — Describe the event in terms of date, logistics, target audience, sponsor's role and anticipated number of participants.

- **Sponsorship request** — This section addresses the amount of the request plus any other expectations of the sponsor (e.g., employee participation, advertising/ promotion, prizes).

- **Sponsor benefits** — List those benefits — both direct and indirect — that you believe would be most appealing to the potential sponsor.

- **Event timeline** — Include an event timeline that encompasses a deadline for the sponsor's response to your request.

Use this sample sponsor proposal to craft your own and secure valuable sponsor support for your next event.

1st Annual Family Wellness Walk
Wanobee YMCA
Sponsorship Proposal Prepared Especially for Acme Insurance

Event Summary

On Sept. 15, the Wanobee YMCA will host its 1st Annual Family Wellness Walk. Our goal is to enlist no fewer than 200 participants who will walk a 10-mile route beginning at the YMCA and conclude at Hagaman Park. Each walking participant will be encouraged to seek pledges based on the number of miles walked. In addition to the event's primary sponsor, 10 additional businesses will be contacted to sponsor each mile along the 10-mile route. Funds raised from the event will be used to develop a fitness trail adjacent to the YMCA and extending two miles to Buttermilk Creek.

Introduction

The Wanobee YMCA was founded in 1958 for the purpose of providing recreational opportunities for Wanobee area residents. Since its founding, the YMCA has expanded its role to improve the lives and quality of life for the families of greater Wanobee and surrounding communities. Proceeds from this event will enable the development of the proposed fitness trail.

Event Description

In addition to generating no less than $25,000, The Wellness Walk will focus attention on the importance of fitness and recreational opportunities. Scheduled to take place on Sept. 15, the event will begin at the YMCA and conclude at Hagaman Park. A 10-member steering committee — with the help of some 40 volunteers — will enlist at least 200 walkers who will be encouraged to secure a minimum of $50 in pledges each ($10,000). In addition, 10 sponsors will be sought to underwrite one mile of the route at $500 each. Each of the 10 sponsors will also be asked to provide volunteers to assist the walkers along the route.

Sponsorship Request

We respectfully invite Acme Insurance to act as the primary sponsor of this year's first annual event — with an investment of $10,000 — knowing that the goal of wellness and improved quality of life is in line with your company's mission. We will publicize that this event is being sponsored by Acme Insurance and invite your employees to take an active role in the event. Our targeted audience will include families throughout greater Wanobee and recognize that this is also a part of your company's primary market. We welcome any opportunities for you to advertise your company during the event. In addition, we will also provide your employees and their families with a free three-day pass to the YMCA.

Wellness Walk Time Line

To proceed with the attached timeline for this special event, we would appreciate your company's response before March 25.

Branding, Varied Activities Ensure a Dazzling Event

The annual fundraiser of the Los Gatos Education Foundation (Los Gatos, CA) needed tweaking. While the event was raising money, the confusion attendees seemed to have about proper attire suggested problems with branding and messaging, says Kimberley Ellery, director of special events.

The solution? Denim and Diamonds.

"The theme really established the tone of the evening," Ellery says. "The décor was casual but elegant — red roses and crystal — and the guests looked fabulous. They were very comfortable in their jeans, but outstanding in their jewelry."

Organizers wove the diamond motif throughout the event, from promotional artwork to a jeweler selling diamonds (and donating a portion of the proceeds to the foundation) at the event itself.

While the theme got people in the door, Ellery credits the variety of activities for securing their support. "We were very deliberate about offering many levels of participation at different price points," says Ellery. "People could jump in for as little as $20, or offer thousands through family sponsorships."

The event's many activities included:

Here's one example of a successful special event that attracted major sponsors as a result of very targeted letters. But be sure to know each business' giving/sponsorship guidelines before submitting each request.

At a Glance —	
Event Type:	Themed Gala
Gross:	$135,000
Costs:	$45,000
Net Income:	$90,000
Volunteers:	6
Planning:	9-12 months
Attendees:	275
Revenue Sources:	Ticket sales, live and silent auctions, blackjack tables, poker tourney, jewelry sales, sponsorships, more
Unique Feature:	Wide variety of activities, price points

- **Chicken Bingo.** A fenced, 7X7-foot grid of 100 squares was brought to the dance floor and attendees bought individual squares for $20. A diamond-wearing chicken was then placed on the grid, and the owner of the square where it did its business won diamond earrings. Of the event Ellery says, "You could have heard a pin drop in that room, everyone was so fascinated. It was a perfect way to focus attention for the auction."

- **Heads or Tails Raffle.** For $30, participants called successive coin flips until only one remained, winning an iPad tablet computer.

- **Premium Wine Bar.** Guests paid $25 per glass to sample fine wine donated by local vineyards. Five-glass punch cards were available for $100.

- **Best of Raffle.** 100 tickets were sold at $100 each, with the winner receiving his or her choice of any single item offered in the live auction.

- **Wine Toss.** For $15 a toss, attendees attempted to ring the necks of donated bottles of wine. Those who succeeded won the wine and an auction item valued at $50 or less. Ellery says, "It's a great way to get rid of leftover bits that can't be easily packaged or auctioned off, packs of five carwash certificates and things like that."

Other activities including a ticketed Texas Hold 'Em tournament, black jack tables, and live and silent auctions helped the event net $90,000.

Source: Kimberley Ellery, Director of Special Events, Los Gatos Education Foundation, Los Gatos, CA. E-mail: KimberleyEllery@comcast.net

Securing Major Corporate Sponsorship

The Denim and Diamonds fundraiser of the Los Gatos Education Foundation (Los Gatos, CA) enjoyed corporate sponsorship from high-profile corporations like OnFulfillment (Newark, CA) and Barracuda Networks (Campbell, CA).

Kimberley Ellery, director of special events, says doing your homework and writing very targeted solicitation letters are critical steps to securing such national-level sponsorships.

"You have to do the research, know exactly what kinds of buckets they donate to and when, and then position yourself firmly in one of those buckets," she says. "Almost all businesses donate somewhere, but most have very strict guidelines about what they do and do not support. So if you want to tap into that level of support, you have to be very clear about how your organization and its event matches their priorities and rules."

Integrate Marketing Initiatives to Secure Sponsorships

With non-dues revenue fast becoming membership organizations' bread and butter, sponsorship opportunities will only grow in importance, says Ann Ormond, president of the Greater Newburyport Chamber of Commerce & Industry (Newburyport, MA), which has a strategy to integrate hardcopy and online presentations of sponsorship opportunities.

Central to the strategy are single-page flyers detailing chamber sponsorship opportunities. Given to potential sponsors, these flyers, such as the two shown below, highlight event activities, key exposure points and sponsorship ranges. Staff also bind a year's worth of flyers into booklets to share with top supporters.

Electronic advertising augments these efforts. Sponsored events are featured in posts that offer a brief description, expected attendance and price range, and a link to the full sponsorship flyer. Ormond estimates website postings generate three to six sponsorships a month while requiring minimal staff time.

To draw potential sponsors, Ormond recommends putting as much critical information up front as possible. "Put the price out front," she says, "and if it's in the ball park, people will call."

She also recommends moving completed events to the bottom of the Web page — not deleting them — to build event awareness.

Source: Ann Ormond, President, Greater Newburyport Chamber of Commerce & Industry, Newburyport, MA.
E-mail: aormond@newburyportchamber.org

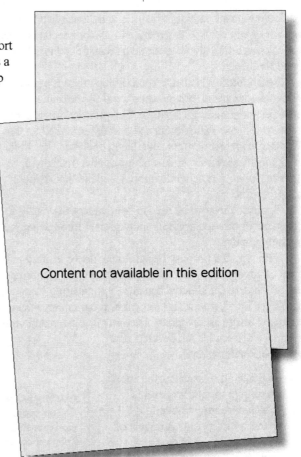

Content not available in this edition

Craft a Corporate Marketing Sponsorship Proposal

Corporate sponsoring relationships need to focus on sponsors' needs, not yours, says Jean Block, of Jean Block Consulting, Inc. (Albuquerque, NM).

"You need to define the sponsorship opportunity in one succinct page," she says. "Corporations, foundations and business sponsors receive millions of these proposals, so yours must have the proper you-me ratio to stand out from other nonprofits' boilerplate proposals."

To determine whether you have a one-size-fits-all proposal, or one that meets the company's needs, conduct the following exercise, says Block:

1. Pull out your existing sponsorship letter and take out a red pen and a green pen (red for stop, green for go).
2. Every time you have written you, your, or the name of the sponsor, circle it with the green marker.
3. Every time you have used we, our, us, my, your organization's name, circle it with the red marker.

"If your sponsorship letter is focused on the sponsor, your proposal will have more green than red," she says. "You know all about you. It's much easier to write about you, and it's much easier to send out one sponsorship letter/packet to everyone. But if you do, you're not going to be successful."

"Marketing is about an exchange. Once you meet their needs you'll get your sponsorship dollars, and you'll get it not by asking for it, but by giving the partner something he or she clearly needs."

Source: Jean Block, Jean Block Consulting, Inc., Albuquerque, NM. E-mail: jean@jblockinc.com.

Put yourself in the shoes of the sponsor when making the ask to ensure you are helping them meet their own business/corporate goals.

WAYS TO APPROACH WOULD-BE SPONSORS

Have You Considered a Sponsorship Menu?

Although you are no doubt familiar with "wish lists" and the ways they can be used to generate funds for needed projects, have you ever developed your own menu of sponsorship opportunities?

Much like a wish list, a sponsorship menu is a printed piece that depicts an organization's gift opportunities for businesses and individuals alike. The primary difference between a sponsorship menu and a wish list is the fact that a sponsorship menu offers advertising opportunities. In fact, many businesses view sponsorships as advertising and, as a result, funding is generally more available than through outright gifts.

Sponsorships can be used to help underwrite existing programs or provide programming not met through a general operating budget.

Although the primary benefit to the donor is often in the form of advertising, both the organization and sponsoring donor can derive additional benefits — sponsoring company employee involvement in the event or program, an enhanced company image as a responsible corporate citizen and more.

Here's how you can develop your own sponsorship menu:

1. Evaluate all of your organization's existing programs and events. Which ones might have sponsorship appeal? A review of your institution's budget may also help reveal potential sponsorship opportunities.

2. Next, brainstorm with employees to identify needs that are not presently being addressed through the budget. Which needs might demonstrate appeal as sponsored programs or events? Put yourself in the place of a would-be sponsor, and ask yourself, "Why would I be interested in sponsoring this program?" Your answer will help determine whether or not it is sponsorship material.

3. List all sponsorship opportunities together and attach a sponsor price-tag to each. Assign an overall sponsorship cost to each program or event and then look for additional sponsor opportunities within each program.

4. After developing a draft menu of sponsorship opportunities, share it with your development committee as well as a handful of nondonors. Ask for their input. What would they change, remove or add to your list? (Sharing this draft selectively will actually help pre-sell items to those involved with the process.)

5. In addition to printing the sponsorship menu, print a simple fact card for each of your larger sponsorship opportunities. Each fact card can delineate lesser sponsorship opportunities within the larger program and spell out specific benefits for the sponsor (e.g., outdoor advertising, signs at the event, pre- and post-publicity, etc.).

Below is a simple example of such a menu you can use as a guide in creating a document that works best for you. Although a sponsorship menu could be incorporated into a direct mail effort, its greatest effectiveness will be realized through face-to-face calls.

MARENGO PUBLIC SCHOOL
2008-09 Sponsorship Opportunities

Marengo Golf/Tennis Classic

Overall sponsor	$10,000
Golf sponsor	$5,000
Tennis sponsor	$2,500
Golf clinic	$750
Tennis clinic	$250
Social hour	$500
Dinner/program	$500
Holes/tees (18)	$120 each

Theatre: Fall performance

Overall sponsor	$2,500
Program sponsor	$500
Post-performance reception	$500

Sponsor a debater

Limit of 20 .... $200 each

The sponsors of this year's debate program will help underwrite travel, lodging and meals associated with our student debate team. You will also be special guests at our Debate Invitational and meet our debaters at a special reception following the event.

For more info: Contact Betsy Swan, 282-0553

Annual lecture series

5 lectures .... $3,000 each

We will host five lectures throughout the year. This year's theme is "values worth protecting." The events are geared to students but open to the public.

Marengo career day

Event sponsor	$1,000
Career panel (5)	$250 each
Luncheon sponsor	$500

Marengo holiday performance

Overall sponsor	$2,000
Holiday reception	$500
Regional tour sponsors	$3,000 each

Marengo Band:
Fall, spring performances

Fall sponsor	$1,000
Spring sponsor	$1,000

Faculty fall retreat $5,000

Each August, Marengo faculty are invited to participate in a three-day professional development and planning session. Outside speakers and facilitators are enlisted for a productive and motivational experience.

For information about athletic sponsorship opportunities, contact Alex Martin: 282-0564

Use Response Cards With Direct Mail, Face-to-face Calls

Every face-to-face or direct mail contact you have with people should allow you to invite their involvement with your organization in some capacity. Whether meeting with a first-time or long-time donor, the business' growing involvement with your institution is the single most important factor in generating new or increased gifts, needed volunteer assistance, or both.

So what systems do you have in place that help to show you when someone may be interested? How do you know when someone might want to establish a scholarship? How do you know someone wants to get involved in planning a special event? When someone is willing to be a sponsor?

The use of response cards or bounce backs should be incorporated whenever and wherever possible. Whenever a new brochure is developed, include an accompanying response card. Whenever correspondence is sent, include a response card. Whenever you meet with anyone, select a response card that best fits the circumstances and share it with the prospect.

The response card gives others a tangible reason to get back to you. And when they do, you don't have to guess or read minds. You have evidence that they have expressed interest in learning more about your organization and perhaps, how they can assist your efforts.

As you can see from the examples here, there is no limit on the number of ways in which you can use this simple tool. Assess the many ways in which bounce backs may be useful in your work.

Incorporate bounce backs into every correspondence you have with potential sponsors (e.g., brochures, annual report, newsletters, etc.).

Examples of bouncebacks that can accompany various types of brochures and mailings.

Pleased to meet you.... Let's get to know each other.

Name _____
Address_____
City _____ State _____ ZIP _____
Daytime Phone _____
Evening Phone _____
Occupation _____ Title _____

I'm interested in learning more about the following:

☐ The college's history and mission.
☐ Distinguishing achievements of the college.
☐ Course offerings/majors.
☐ Career advising.
☐ Financial aid/scholarship assistance.
☐ Upcoming calendar of events.
☐ Speakers bureau topics.
☐ Volunteer opportunities.
☐ Exploring planned gift opportunities.
☐ Annual fund opportunities.
☐ Endowed gift opportunities.
☐ How to establish a scholarship.
☐ The college's future plans.
☐ Alumni activities and involvement.
☐ Distinguished graduates of the institution.
☐ Status of the endowment.
☐ Other_____

Learn More About How to Establish a Scholarship

Name _____
Address_____
City _____ State _____ ZIP _____
Daytime Phone _____
Evening Phone _____
Occupation _____ Title _____

I would like to learn more about establishing or adding to a named scholarship. Please provide me with additional information on the following topic(s):

☐ How scholarships help students.
☐ How scholarships help the college.
☐ How scholarships help our society.
☐ How to establish a named scholarship.
☐ Using memorial gifts to establish a _____ scholarship.
☐ Annual scholarships and how they work.
☐ Endowed scholarships and how they work.
☐ Placing restrictions on scholarships.
☐ Establishing or adding to a scholarship through my estate.
☐ Selection of scholarship recipients.
☐ Meeting the recipients of my scholarship.
☐ Potential tax benefits of establishing a scholarship.

Last Year's Cutbacks Become This Year's Funding Opportunities

If your organization has experienced specific budget cutbacks due to the economy or other factors over which you have no control, don't overlook those items as funding opportunities for sponsors who want to see their gifts making a noticeable difference.

Take the time to review each budget line item or program axed last year and evaluate its potential as a sponsorship opportunity for the current year. After identifying a range of projects with varying costs, produce a "bring them back" wish list you can selectively share with individuals and businesses that may choose to fund one or more of them.

The difference between a traditional wish list and a "bring them back" list is the fact that a wish list identifies needs that have yet to be realized and a "bring them back" list identifies more crucial needs that were, until last year, part of your general operations.

It is important to point out to past contributors, however, that any gifts directed to the "bring them back" list be in addition to what they normally contribute. This, in effect, would be a way to upgrade existing sponsors. This obviously would not apply to previous nondonors since any gift they make would provide "new" money.

Consider making a list of budget cutbacks as possible sponsorship opportunities available to business or individual prospects.

Below is a sample illustration you can use as a template to create a "bring them back" wish list of your own.

'Bring Them Back' Gift Opportunities
Hatfield Crisis Center

Below is a list of actual programs and expenditures that, until this year, had been a vital part of the crisis center. Due to significant government funding cutbacks, however, these programs, personnel and annual expenditures had to be eliminated in order to project a balanced budget for the current fiscal year. The need for these items is imperative; however, it is equally important that the crisis center operate within its means.

We invite you to "bring back" one or more of these budget cutback items by making a restricted contribution in addition to whatever you have given in previous years. (Unfortunately, simply redirecting your past level of support to a project would have no net impact on the budget.)

Thank you for helping us regain our footing in assisting those in need.

PERSONNEL OPPORTUNITIES

Director of outreach services — For four years, we have made a noticeable difference in reaching out to individuals and families facing domestic abuse and violence issues who were unaware of our services. In many instances, this staff member's work helped in preventing catastrophic consequences.   *Replacement Cost* $27,000

Outreach services budget — These funds were being used to cover necessary costs associated with the director's position — travel, phone, transportation of those in need, temporary housing and other administrative costs.   *Replacement Cost* $12,000

PROGRAM OPPORTUNITIES

Job placement program — This program, in place for eight years, helped find job opportunities for women who, in many instances, were on their own for the first time and working to fully support themselves.   *Replacement Cost* $11,000

SPECIFIC BUDGET LINE ITEMS

Hope newsletter — Cut back from four quarterly issues to two. Printing and postage reductions.   *Replacement Cost* $1,100

Facility maintenance budget — Cut back by 10 percent.
              Replacement Cost $840

Professional development/training — Overall training/professional development for all personnel was cut back by 30 percent.   *Replacement Cost* $1,500

Be Prepared for First-time Visits

How prepared are you when calling on a business for the first time? Have you attempted to find out anything about its past giving history? Do you know which organizations the business has supported in recent years? Use this checklist to prepare yourself for first-time calls on businesses:

- ❑ To what causes has the business contributed in the past year(s)?

- ❑ What are its top funding interests?

- ❑ Who are the decision makers with regard to contributions?

- ❑ When does its fiscal year begin and end?

- ❑ What are the business' primary products/services?

- ❑ Are gifts made on an ongoing basis or at regular intervals?

- ❑ Does the business have a policy with regard to gifts and sponsorships that is public?

- ❑ What process is followed for submitting sponsorship requests?

- ❑ How is the overall financial well-being of the company?

- ❑ Does our organization have any board members, donors or others who also have a relationship with this company?

- ❑ What are the similarities and differences between this company's philosophy and that of our organization?

Diminish the anxiety of first-time visits by doing your homework. Knowing the answers to these questions will help calm those nerves when approaching businesses for the first time.

Set the Stage for 'Cold Calls' With an Introductory Letter

Veteran development professionals will tell you that the best method for making contact with new prospects is through a mutual introduction by someone close to both the business/corporation and your organization. As helpful as that method can be, there are obviously times when that cannot occur. In those instances, it's better to attempt a cold call than to make no contact at all.

When it's necessary to make a cold call on a prospect, is it best to show up unannounced, hoping to gain an audience? Or should you attempt to set an appointment first? While there may be some exceptions to the rule, setting an appointment is generally the wisest move. After all, if the business in question has absolutely no interest in meeting you, it's a waste of their and your time to make the attempt.

Before calling for an appointment, however, it's best to send a personal letter of introduction — one that will set the stage for your upcoming call. Such a letter will make the case for your visit and generally improve your odds of securing an appointment. Additionally, a letter of introduction will add credibility to you and the cause you represent.

Develop a letter of introduction similar to the example at right as a first step in attempting to set an appointment with the new prospect.

Dear <Name>:

I am writing with the hope that you will give me 30 minutes of your time to introduce myself and visit with you about The Boys and Girls Home and its role in our community.

I know that your business has a long and successful history in our community and I respect the level of involvement and leadership you have taken in community affairs over the years. The Boys and Girls Home has also had a long history of service to this community, and, for that reason, I believe you and I have some mutual interests.

While it is my genuine hope that you consider a contribution to The Boys and Girls Home, I ask that you meet with me briefly regardless of any decision regarding a gift. I want you to be aware of some of the exciting achievements our organization is making, and ask for your input regarding a future project we are exploring.

I will contact you within the next 10 days to arrange an appointment. Thank you in advance for granting me this opportunity to meet with you.

Sincerely,
<Name>

WAYS TO APPROACH WOULD-BE SPONSORS

Make Your Introductory Call an Attention Grabber

Whenever making a first-time call on a new prospect or business, avoid starting out your presentation with a brief history of your organization. Everyone has heard that approach, and it's frankly a boring way to begin building rapport with someone you hope will contribute to your organization. Instead, develop a menu of introductory approaches from which you can choose. Here are three different ways to open your conversation:

1. **Begin by pointing out accomplishments.** Describe one or two significant ways in which your organization has contributed to the welfare of your community or region.

2. **Share a startling fact.** Furnish the prospect with a fact that legitimizes the existence and work of your nonprofit: "It's estimated that one in five children in our county still doesn't have access to computers." Then move into what your organization is doing to address that challenge.

3. **Point out mutually beneficial interests.** Share information that helps the business to realize that it's in their best interest to support you. For example, you might zero in on your organization's economic impact to the community: "We have determined that, based on the number of visitors we bring to town, some $5 million is annually spent with local businesses."

Although you can always get into your organization's history and other useful information at some point in this introductory conversation, it's important for the prospect to know early on that the time he/she is giving up for your visit is justified.

Talk the Talk and Walk the Walk

Business professionals appreciate businesslike behavior. Keep the following tips in mind when meeting with a CEO or other corporate executives:

- **Dress professionally.** The first impression is important, so err on the side of conservative attire.
- **Be punctual.** Time is money, and business persons can't afford to wait. Be on time for all meetings. If you're going to be late, notify the appropriate person in advance.
- **Bring a copy of your group's annual report.** It doesn't have to be flashy, but it should have a clear financial statement. Be prepared to answer questions and provide reasons for why the company should give to your organization.
- **Don't take up too much time.** If set to meet for an hour, respect that commitment.
- **Respond quickly to requests** for additional information.
- **Thank those involved** for their time and positive consideration.

Develop a Routine for Setting Appointments

It's so easy to get caught up in "administrative" demands — internal meetings, paperwork, etc. — that staff may often give less attention to making sponsorship calls than anticipated. To ensure you get out of the office on a regular basis, develop a procedure that ensures you are making a minimum number of calls every week.

Here is one example of how to set aside time for scheduling appointments:

Earmark every Tuesday and Thursday afternoon for appointment-setting. Let others know that this time is off limits for meetings and unscheduled visits. Review your list of business prospects and schedule phone calls to get appointments locked up for the next two-week period. Try to protect your Tuesday and Thursday afternoons so they will remain available as future appointment-setting periods.

By having two designated times per week for setting appointments, you will have two opportunities to attempt to reach prospects should you be unable to reach them the first time. Also, should something unexpected prevent you from scheduling calls on one of those two times, you still have a last opportunity to do some scheduling.

Vary your introduction to would-be sponosrs to test which approaches work best for you.

You cannot take back a first impression, so make it count!

Refer to Your Nonprofit's Economic Impact

When seeking support from businesses, know that they are more likely to support those nonprofits that positively impact your community's economy. They want to know how their gifts will help the business climate. That's why it is worth your time to study and know your organization's impact on the local and regional economy. You can use those results in making your case for gift support from businesses.

When conducting an economic impact study, involve key members of your business community as one way to engage them in the life and work of your organization. They can play a significant role in publicizing the results of your study to others.

Answers to these and other questions may provide compelling reasons for businesses to support your annual fundraising efforts.

Use your organization's economic impact on the community to help make your case for gift support from businesses.

- ✓ Where does your organization rank in relation to other employers in terms of number of employees, employee payroll and overall budget?

- ✓ How do your services positively impact the economy? Do they save the community money? Do they generate revenue or jobs?

- ✓ How would the absence of your nonprofit negatively impact the economy?

Sample Economic Impact Studies

Below is a sampling of economic impact studies:

Bucknell University (Lewisburg, PA)
(www.bucknell.edu/x6222.xml)

Harvard University (Cambridge, MA)
(www.community.harvard.edu/economic.php)

Nonprofit Alliance of Monterey County (Salinas, CA)
(www.alliancemonterey.org/PDFs/econ_report_32pgs.pdf)

Midland Lutheran College (Fremont, NE)
(www.mlc.edu) — Click on "News & Information," then "Archived News Items" and choose "Study shows Midland serves as a vital partner in local economy"

South Carolina Public Library
(www.libsci.sc.edu/SCEIS/home.htm)

Three Rules for Meeting With Decision Makers

Before you can make your case, you need to get decision makers to agree to meet with you. Boost your chances for success with these three appointment-setting guidelines:

1. **Should you make the call yourself or have an assistant do it?** Make the call yourself. Your purpose for the call is to develop rapport with the prospect. The call lays the foundation for what will happen at the meeting.

2. **When planning a trip, how hard should you push for a meeting?** If you're traveling to a certain area, identify two sets of dates on which your could meet before setting up appointments with prospects. That way, if the prospect says he/she is busy on the first date, you can say, "I also plan to be in your area on (date). Could we meet then?" It will be difficult for the prospect to say "no" twice.

3. **What should you do if you get an answering machine?** If, after several attempts, you still can't connect, leave a message. "This is (name). I'm calling for (institution name). I'm going to be in town on (date) and would like to talk about the exciting things happening at (institution name). Please call me back at (phone number), so we can set a time that works best for you."

Appointment-setting Tips

- Use networking events to lay the groundwork for setting an appointment. For example: "May I call your secretary to set up an appointment that will work with your schedule?" Getting prior approval for a meeting avoids leaving you at the mercy of the "gatekeeper."

- Third-party endorsement approach — "We've recently had several businesses take a closer look at becoming sponsors of some of our events, including Acme Printing, which chose to sponsor this year's traveling art exhibit. I would like to schedule a 20-minute meeting with you just to share some available sponsorship opportunities."

Dos and Don'ts to Boost Your Sponsorship Revenue

Corporate sponsorship is one of the largest single sources of revenue in special event and program-based fundraising. It is also one of the most volatile, capable of fluctuating widely from year to year — both up and down.

Winning the support of corporate partners requires mutual trust and a close alignment of interests, but a few time-tested pointers can make a big difference. To help you make the most of your outreach efforts, Jean Block, president of Jean Block Consulting Inc. (Albuquerque, NM), offers the following lists of sponsorship solicitation dos and don'ts.

Seek sponsors a year in advance by incorporating all sponsorship opportunities into one letter.

DON'T:

- Address a request to "Dear Friend." Do your homework and find out who should receive your request.
- Ask the Right Sponsor for the Wrong Thing. Research the sponsor's marketing priorities.
- Ask the Right Sponsor at the Wrong Time. Research their giving cycles.
- Whine at the companies who turn you down. Instead, politely ask them for suggestions on how to improve your proposal.
- Be too busy to write thank-you letters (especially creative ones).
- Assume you are the only one asking. Develop a way to show how you are different from or better than other nonprofits.
- Toss the sponsor's guidelines aside and submit only what you want. There are reasons for the sponsor's questions.
- Go around the person whose responsibility it is to deal with your request.
- Only contact the sponsor when you want money.
- Keep calling — constantly — to check on the progress of your proposal.

DO:

- Look for ways to collaborate with other organizations if you can. Combine your requests for higher impact.
- Seize an opportunity to follow up with sponsors. Send a quarterly progress report –get them involved in the success of your event.
- Ask the sponsor how to show your appreciation. Be sure that you deliver what you promise. Take pictures. Value the sponsor's investment.
- Make a personal visit to the potential sponsor before a significant request, take an influential board member or volunteer. Interview the sponsor, ask questions and listen to the sponsor's requests.
- Be creative with your request. Money isn't the only thing sponsors have to offer. Look for in-kind opportunities.
- Give more than adequate leadtime for the sponsor to respond to your request. Research giving cycles.
- Thank the potential sponsor for their consideration, even if you are turned down — remember that you are building a relationship for the future.
- Ask for references of other sponsors who might be interested in your program or project.
- Do a quality control check — Be sure you have spelled the sponsor's name correctly, have the right title, address, etc.

Determine what component of your special event will most appeal to a prospect and tailor your proposal to that aspect of the event.

Block, who spent years on the corporate side of corporate philanthropy, says these steps may sound simple, but they can have a powerful effect on your fundraising efforts. Following these simple steps, she says will distinguish your organization from the great majority of nonprofit sponsorship-seekers and help you secure much-needed sponsorship dollars.

Source: Jean Block, President, Jean Block Consulting Inc., Albuquerque, NM.
E-mail: jean@jblockinc.com.

Discuss Ways
Of Overcoming Prospect Objections

During one of your upcoming staff meetings, schedule some time to discuss possible comebacks for sponsorship objections.

Present a list of objections your staff has heard in the past and then spend some time reviewing each objection and brainstorming comebacks they might use in the future. Record the responses so you can develop a written "objection comebacks" sheet (such as the one shown here), the staff can review and memorize.

Allow your team to commiserate over past call experiences and collectively discuss and create responses to prospect objections. You may even wish to spend some time prioritizing comebacks.

Here is an example of a worksheet that examines potential objections to sponsorship requests and your responses so that you are ready to address reasons prospects give you as to why they can't support your organization at this time.

Prospect Objection Comebacks	
Prospect Objections	Possible Comeback
I really don't have any ties to your organization.	
I have other philanthropic interests.	
When you get rid of (name of employee), I might think about giving.	
I don't like the way you folks handled....	
You don't do enough business with me.	
That's too much.	
You folks are always asking for money.	
Your organization is too liberal (or conservative) for my way of thinking.	

Making Presentations
To Corporate Gift Committees

The key to making a successful presentation to a corporate gifts committee is developing a strong relationship between your nonprofit and the key decision makers at the corporation. Tailor your presentation to those key decision makers — usually the CEO and/or the head of the corporate giving committee — because if you have them on your side, it doesn't matter who else is involved.

Here are some tips for making presentations to corporate gift committees:

✓ Align the content of your presentation with the corporation's priorities.

✓ Let them know beforehand the format that you will use to make your presentation (e.g., Will you use PowerPoint? How much time will you allow for Q&A? Will you provide handouts?).

Ask Sponsors
To Help With Raffle Prizes

Ease the burden of trying to get your raffle prizes donated by asking businesses to sponsor big-ticket items. Many places that sell these items most likely have been tapped for donations. Use the business relationships you or your board members have to ask them to donate the item instead. You can recognize the business on the event's program or print their name on the raffle ticket.

Corporate Call Tip

■ Even if someone in a company's middle management serves as the point person for initial sponsorship requests, consider relying on a board member or other insider to make a first contact with the company's CEO. That way, when you approach the middle manager to set an appointment or submit a proposal, you can use the CEO's name in your message: "We have chatted with your boss about this project and she asked us to share it with you."

Don't shy away from using the point person's name when setting an appointment with the key decision maker.

Equip Volunteer Callers With Solicitation Summary Reports

Use of call reports to track conversations with potential sponsors can lead you to a sponsorship commitment six months to a year later.

What documentation do you provide volunteers to help them make effective calls on your charity's behalf?

Volunteers and board members can be instrumental in soliciting gifts of all kinds — annual, major gifts, planned gifts and more. Their effectiveness, however, is a measure of how well-equipped they are before, during and after a call is made.

The solicitation summary report shown here serves as a valuable tool for volunteer solicitors. The one-page tool is intended to:

1. Provide a concise summary of the prospect along with his/her recent giving history.

2. Give specific instructions regarding type of call to be made.

3. Encourage the caller to record when the call was made, what took place and what follow-up steps should occur.

Although volunteers and board members involved in the solicitation process should receive appropriate training prior to making calls, the solicitation summary report becomes an important tool both prior to and following the call. Prospect profile information and instructions are valuable to the volunteer, and comments and follow-up advice are useful to staff and future volunteers involved with a particular call.

The following information is intended to help you better instruct volunteers as to the form's use:

1. **Prospect profile** — basic information intended to help the volunteer understand the individual's relationship with the charity and establish rapport with him/her.

2. **Objective** — provides a clear statement of expectation for the volunteer.

3. **Call outcome** — volunteer summarizes the call: To what degree the stated objective was met, along with any comments that may provide insight into the prospect's decision.

4. **Follow-up** — describes what future steps should be carried out (and when), based on the call's outcome.

5. **Volunteer's signature and date** report is turned in to the charity's office.

Use this template to create an agency-specific solicitation summary report to help volunteers make effective calls on your organization's behalf.

SOLICITATION SUMMARY REPORT

Prospect Name _____ Title _____

Organization _____

Address_____

Phone (W) _____ (H)_____

Relationship to [Name of Charity] _____

_____

Solicitation Target_____

Recent Giving History _____

Objective of Call _____

Name of Solicitor _____

Date of Call_____ Duration of Call _____

Met with Prospect at:
☐ Office   ☐ Residence   ☐ Other_____

Summary of Call's Outcome _____

_____

_____

_____

Recommended Follow-up_____

_____

_____

_____

_____   _____

SIGNATURE OF SOLICITOR   DATE

Keep Testing New Calling Approaches

When calling on businesses for support, see if this approach sounds all too familiar: Establish rapport, make small talk, build the case for support then make the ask to sponsor an upcoming event/project.

Instead of the "same old, same old," why not vary your approach? In addition to being a lot less boring, doing so lets you test different presentation techniques and funding opportunities to see what works best. Here's some of what you can test:

1. **Make team calls** rather than making all calls alone. Bring a board member along on some calls one day. Try asking your mayor to accompany you on some calls. Ask a respected CEO or someone served by your organization if she/he would accompany you on three calls.

2. **Say it differently.** Deliver your presentation in various ways to see what works best and to break up the monotony. Compare the prospect's business to your organization. Share a dream of what could be. Use story telling to build a compelling case for support.

3. **Try different "props."** Rather than leaving behind the standard sponsorship proposal, try something new. Share a handful of photos that help the prospect visualize the gift opportunity. Share a brief recording.

4. **Vary your funding projects.** In addition to special events, define specific projects that might interest prospects more: sponsoring a particular program, enhancing a supplies budget, providing professional development funds for your employees, etc.

Soliciting Tips...

Next time you're preparing to make a solicitation call, consider these points:

- Rather than getting a prospect to think about an amount of money to give, get them to think about a project that costs money.
- Before making the call, ask yourself three times "why" the prospect should make this gift. (It's like a warm up exercise that will put you in the right frame of mind).
- Try to anticipate a prospect's objections by answering them in your presentation.

Don't Overlook Sponsors' Employees

Anytime you convince a business to step forward and help sponsor an event, be sure to involve their employees as well. Examples include:

- Selling tickets
- Delivering drinks
- Setting up and cleaning up
- Hosting and greeting
- Conducting tours
- Transportation and parking
- Registration
- Answering phones

You may even see opportunities to incorporate fun competition and prizes into employees' involvement.

Sponsorship Tips...

- When approaching a potential sponsor, explain that you want to give him/her the first opportunity to sponsor the entire event (or project) before inviting others.

    It saves time if you can get one business to cover the total cost rather than sharing it among a group of sponsors.

- Before approaching a potential sponsor, anticipate possible objections and write them down. Then develop a list of responses for each objection.

Don't Confine Yourself to Once-a-year Calls on Businesses

Have you ever gotten this response when calling on a business? "The only time I hear from you is when you're asking me for money."

You're not alone. It happens to lots of fundraisers who are expected to make so many calls that it becomes challenging to have contacts with businesses beyond the normal once-a-year ask. But even so, there are actions you can take to nurture your organization's relationship with business donors and donor hopefuls.

Here's a sampling of some of the cultivation (and stewardship) moves you can take between solicitation calls:

- Make mention of a group of business supporters every time your internal newsletter is distributed. Then send a copy of it to the business with a note saying: "Our employees know you're an investor here, and they appreciate it!"

- Clip news items of interest and send them to your business contact along with a personal note: "Just thought you might find this to be of interest...."

- Hold one or more invitation-only receptions at your facility during the year for both business contributors and prospects.

- Ask board members and development committee volunteers to begin making thank-you calls on business contributors two or three months prior to your annual solicitation call.

- Send a mid-year note or make a mid-year phone call pointing out how that business' gift is making a difference for those you serve.

Sponsor Stewardship Should be an Ongoing Effort

Take the time to get to know your sponsors. Share information about the project company officials are funding. Ask for their input. Find out what more you can do, within reason, to make them pleased with the collaboration.

An important part of maintaining a strong relationship with sponsors is to make them your fans all year long.

Steward your sponsors just as you would all major donors.

Keep Sponsors Year to Year by Offering Right of First Refusal

As a sponsorship benefit, sponsors of the annual conference for the Association of Air Medical Services (Alexandria, VA) have right of first refusal on future conference sponsorships.

"Right of first refusal" means that the association will contact the sponsoring company prior to allowing someone else to pick up on the sponsorship for the coming year, says Blair Marie Beggan, communications and marketing manager.

"Once a company has sponsored any item or special event for one year," Beggan says, "they always have the option to renew the sponsorship for the following year before it is offered as an option to another company."

Offering the right of first refusal to current sponsors means those sponsors don't have to keep track of the sponsorships they want to support because they know that the association will contact them each year, says Beggan.

"Offering the right of first refusal helps to build long-term relationships between our organization and our corporate members," she says. "As a small nonprofit, we simply could not hold such a robust and quality conference without the partnerships with our corporate sponsors."

To remind sponsors of their right of first refusal, Beggan calls each sponsor to gauge interest level for the upcoming year.

About 90 percent of their sponsors take advantage of the right of first refusal benefit, she says: "Our niche industry is fairly close-knit. I have the luxury of one-on-one relationships with all of my sponsors. It is rare to have a sponsor drop out of the program. Even in the economic downturn over the past year, only two opted out of their sponsorship, and in one of those cases, I was able to work with them to find something that would be a better fit for their budget."

Source: Blair Marie Beggan, Communications & Marketing Manager, Association of Air Medical Services, Alexandria, VA . E-mail: bbeggan@aams.org

Publicize Prior Year's Sponsors in a Big Way

As you near the end of a fiscal year, decide on ways to publicize all of your past year's sponsors in highly visible ways. Why? Two reasons:

1) One last thank you gives current sponsors an extra measure of recognition and will help to retain them as future sponsors; and

2) Bringing visibility to current sponsors plants seeds in would-be sponsors' minds.

Purchase a full-page newspaper ad to publicly thank all your prior year's sponsors. Hold a press conference with last year's sponsors in attendance. At your next big event, invite all sponsors as special guests and ask them to stand and be recognized.

Your year-end thank you will lay the groundwork as you plan to re-approach them and will also give a heads up to would-be sponsors you plan to approach.

In addition to thanking your sponsors at the conclusion of an event, thank them at year's end.

Have You Considered a Club for All Sponsors?

You no doubt have special clubs for annual contributors who give at certain levels. Chances are you also have a special society for all planned gift donors.

But what about a club for all individuals and businesses that sponsor events and programs throughout the year?

Why not bring even more attention to your sponsors by creating a special alliance that caters to all sponsors for the current fiscal year? In addition to the more individualized perks you offer sponsors, a club such as this would allow for group-related functions and also help motivate others to become sponsors.

Take Steps to Retain Sponsors From Year to Year

It's obviously more cost effective to retain a sponsor from year to year than to try to secure replacements. That's why it's important to steward existing sponsors throughout the year.

Some of what you can do to retain sponsors from year to year includes:

1. Finding ways to show them the impact their support has on your organization and those you serve.

2. Exploring multi-year sponsorships that may offer more perks than the normal yearly sponsorship.

3. Getting others involved (e.g., your CEO, board members, employees) in praising and expressing appreciation to sponsors at various times throughout the year.

Be the Best at Honoring Event Sponsors

The ways in which you recognize sponsors will not only impact their future sponsorship decisions, but also would-be sponsors.

Choose from an array of recognition actions that will help your nonprofit stand out among others. These forms of recognition may include the following actions:

- Special seating and public recognition at events.
- Advertisements geared toward targeted audiences.
- Feature stories on your sponsors in your own publications and in the public media.
- Perks (e.g., tickets) for the sponsoring company's employees.
- Invitation to a preview party.
- Prominent recognition in all printed materials.
- Prominent signage at key locations.
- Letters of thanks from board members, your CEO, those served by your nonprofit and others.
- Evaluation interview and report following the program or event.

Sponsorship Tips

■ If one of your top sponsors decides not to participate next year, don't start over from scratch trying to find a replacement. First, go to those who have traditionally sponsored projects/programs at lower levels. Try to upgrade them. If they agree, it will be easier to find a replacement for whatever they were sponsoring.

■ It's much easier to retain a sponsor from year to year than to recruit a new one. It's also much more time and cost effective to retain sponsors.

Here's one way to retain a sponsor: Within six weeks following the conclusion of your event (or whatever the business or corporation sponsored), meet with your sponsor contact to report on the success of this year's event and then re-enlist the sponsor for next year.

STEWARDING & RETAINING SPONSORS

From Prospects to Sponsors to Major Donors

Recognize that today's sponsors will likely become tomorrow's major donors.

Contributions from companies can be pursued via a number of different avenues. The direct request to the corporate contributions contact may not always be the easiest nor most effective means to generate a gift. Sometimes companies prefer the visibility and opportunities which occur through sponsorships and charitable partnerships. If you plan your approaches well, this form of fundraising can be very successful and beneficial for a variety of reasons.

Recruiting Sponsors

- The first step in your plan should be to determine which companies would make good partners for your organization. Start by looking at your vendors, area retailers, manufacturers with local ties, financial institutions and so on.
- Before you approach a company, know their interests and how they want to be tied to your community. Find out about their marketing objectives and the image they want to project. See how your organization can fit into those objectives.
- Sponsorships and venture partnerships usually are funded from marketing and advertising budgets, instead of through contributions departments or committees, so there may be money available in these "pockets" which you might not otherwise be able to get.
- People give to people, so get to know the right contacts in the companies. If you will be dealing with the marketing or human resources departments for these partnerships, that is where you need to start building relationships. Discover the interests of the individuals and how those interests affect the decisions of the companies.

Donation Sources

- A fairly traditional method of getting companies involved in your organization is to invite them to sponsor special events such as gala dinners, tournaments and so on. Design a menu of choices with various sponsorship levels, and include different perks for each level. Generally, the higher level donors receive items such as better tables, more tickets for their employees, event signage and advertising in event brochures. Make sure your promotional material lists what the sponsors will get for their money, and indicate the nondeductible portions in your receipts.
- Grand openings can generate funds for your organization if the companies agree to give you a percentage of their profits during the celebration. One incentive for the companies is that they can generate more interest in the stores by using your mailing list for invitations than they would through regular advertising.
- Similar to the grand openings approach, a number of companies offer special promotions during which they donate profit percentages. These may be in conjunction with anniversaries, holiday sales, new subscriber drives and the like, and generally involve a marketing campaign which promotes the charity.
- Some companies contribute portions of their sales on specific products throughout the year. Their packaging may even include information about the charity.
- With the explosion of the Internet and the World Wide Web, the opportunities for partnerships with corporations continue to expand. Companies and charities can include links to each others' Web pages, and some technology companies may even offer their services and resources to create Internet sites for nonprofit organizations.

Moving From Sponsor to Major Donor

- High level corporate donors often start out as sponsors. Often, it is easier to initiate them to your organization through lower level sponsorships where they get something for their donations. The employees may have an interest in golf or want to attend special dinners, and this is a good way to get them interested in your organization.
- One way to move a company up in its giving level is to show how the sponsorship has given them an image boost. If they get something from the partnership, even on an intangible level, they are more likely to continue it and allow it to grow.
- Challenge the companies to beat their previous year's contributions. As their sponsorship level continues to go higher each year, it will be a natural path to major donor giving.

Six Ways to Recognize Event Sponsors

Thanking major event sponsors can be an ongoing process that not only recognizes them on the big day, but seeks to solidify their partnership with your cause throughout the year in a variety of ways. To give your sponsors the recognition they deserve:

1. **Include them in entertainment.** Provide your event emcee with names and a few fun details about key supporters to be worked into a monologue. When Bette Midler tours, for example, she weaves comments about local mayors, business leaders and news-makers into her audience banter.

2. **Offer sponsor gift packages.** These may include hotel lodging and dinners when overnight stays are required, restaurant gift certificates, spa visits and a chauffeur. For local supporters, a theme gift basket of gourmet foods, fragrances and candles or other specialty items is always welcome.

3. **Provide company logo recognition and promotion.** Use banners with patterns of sponsor logos as backdrops wherever photos or video will be taken, project the images on stage screens or overhead television monitors along with your own logo.

4. **Include sponsor features in souvenir programs.** Even if the company already bought an ad, write a feature article about its charitable work that tells a more personal story than an advertisement could.

5. **Spread the news online.** Prominently feature event sponsors on your organization's website with their logos and links to the company website. You could also give them their own page on your site where supporters can learn more about the business's phil-anthropic side. Include their logo and company link in all e-mails related to the event.

6. **Engage sponsors as spokespersons.** Take every possible opportunity to thank sponsors publicly and give them a chance to say kind words about your mission, too. For example, ask a representative of your sponsor's company to join you on radio or television programs where you promote the event, giving this person a chance to say why the company supports your organization.

Sponsorship recognition doesn't have to end with signage and logo placement. Think outside the box when looking to honor those who have stepped forward to underwrite your events or programs.

Recognize Your Event's Corporate Sponsors

You have the good fortune to have a noted corporate sponsor for your next event. Showcasing your partnership helps elevate esteem for both of you. Consider these approaches for involving them in as many high profile ways as possible:

✓ **Name a major service award for the corporation.** If your event includes recognizing key people in your organization, ask the corporate CEO to present the "XYZ Company Spirit Award" to a top honoree.

✓ **Ask company staff to be judges or announcers.** Your event may have scholarship presentations, prize drawings, an art show with awards or a major auction item. Be sure representatives from the corporation are front and center when all eyes are on that activity.

✓ **Ask them to help you identify ways to promote them.** The direct approach can be the most effective. A brainstorming session with the corporate sponsor's communications staff may uncover some fresh strategies that will come from two distinct viewpoints — theirs and yours.

✓ **Use their facility for your event.** Your sponsor may have wide green lawns, a spacious atrium, auditorium or dining facility that is ideal for your occasion. More than simply asking that they underwrite food and beverage costs, give them the chance to open their doors and introduce themselves to the community.

✓ **Include them in public service announcements (PSAs).** Ask one of your sponsor's key staff members to make your television or radio PSAs, using an introduction like "Hello, I'm Pat Adams, CEO of XYZ. I hope to see you at the Community Hospital Spring Run for MS awareness. ..."

Give your sponsors a special identity of their own.

ADDITIONAL STRATEGIES FOR SECURING SPONSORSHIPS

Ask the Right Questions for Better Sponsor Results

Submit key questions to know your event or program will make the best match with a would-be sponsor.

You want your sponsors to connect with your organization on a personal level, to feel engaged in your mission. Sponsors, in turn, want bang for their buck.

So how do you accomplish both important goals? By making sure sponsors feel listened to, know they're making a difference and are receiving benefits from sponsorships.

Ask potential sponsors these questions to be sure they are a good match for your special event and your organization's cause:

- **What would make this sponsorship worthwhile for you?** This simple question is often the most overlooked. It is also the most important. Ask this question and then listen, intently. Then, follow through on what they say. If sponsors say they don't care about a plaque to hang in their lobby as long as they have 10 minutes to speak at the event, make that happen.

- **How involved do you want to be?** Some sponsors want personal contact and interaction with the people they're helping; others may be uncomfortable with that. Make sure you know up front how much involvement they want to ensure what level of contact they seek is something you are able to deliver.

- **Who are the key contact people?** Who needs to give logo approval? Who needs to sign off on budgetary issues? Who needs to give the OK on the CEO's speech? Save everyone time and energy by knowing who to contact about what.

- **When would be a good time to follow up next year?** Especially if you get a "no" because the timing of your ask is off, make sure you know when the company plans its philanthropic budget.

Don't overlook putting together a sponsor results package once your event is over. This will put the results of the sponsor's contributions in black and white and set the stage for future support.

Create a Sponsor Results Package

Every potential sponsor has one question on their minds when being pitched: Is this worth my marketing dollars? How can you make sure this question is answered to their satisfaction? By creating a sponsor results package. The following steps will help you make that sponsor a repeat sponsor.

- **Get it in writing.** Make sure the sponsor has a written document acknowledging what they are receiving for their investment.

- **Keep it on hand.** Make sure you keep that document handy during the course of the campaign or the planning and execution of the event. Every time you fulfill a commitment or secure an additional opportunity for them, mark it down.

- **Document, document, document.** Secure clippings of any print articles, copies of any radio or TV broadcast coverage and track numbers of impressions and, most important, the monetary value of those impressions.

When the campaign or event is over, put all of the materials together in a logo folder or, if necessary, a professional looking binder. Have a member of your board and/or your CEO hand deliver the package to the sponsor, along with a small recognition piece.

Keep a copy of all the documentation for your own records. These things will help you the next time you pitch that same sponsor.

ADDITIONAL STRATEGIES FOR SECURING SPONSORSHIPS

Partner With Other Nonprofits When All Else Fails

If you have repeatedly struck out with particular corporations or businesses, you might want to try a group approach.

Get together other nonprofits in your community or region to craft a joint sponsorship proposal that can be equally divided among those making the group request.

Perhaps you can jointly address a challenge facing your community to which each organization can respond in various ways based on their missions and services. One group of nonprofits, made up of a domestic violence center, a girls' club and a library, developed a proposal that focused on child neglect issues. The sponsorship was to be used by each participating organization to address preventative measures.

Some donors — particularly businesses and corporations — are attracted to causes offering gift opportunities that go beyond the scope of one organization.

Take the lead. Approach other nonprofit development officers and, together, explore common funding possibilities.

Many would-be sponsors are attracted to collaborative efforts. Partner with other organizations to reach out to new sponsors.

Nonprofit Leverages $1,500 Sponsorship Into $10,000

Officials at Family Support Line (Media, PA) wanted to add a raffle to their annual auction, but faced a dilemma. A high profile prize like a car or trip would draw interest but drive ticket prices too high. But smaller-scale raffles had fizzled in the past. (The organization also lacked connections to acquire a big-ticket prize).

The solution turned out to be as simple as pulling into the local filling station.

"Raffles are all about having a product that appeals to the widest possible constituency, and gas prices were really hurting people at the time," says Christine Linvill, assistant director. "Free gasoline is extremely usable, and was something we felt would be very attractive at a ticket price of $5."

Auction organizers approached a regional chain of convenience store/gas stations that had been a long-time supporter of the event, and made a simple request: instead of its usual $1,500 sponsorship of the auction, would it be willing to give $1,500 worth of raffleable gifts cards?

The sponsor was onboard from the beginning, says Linvill. "It was a great marketing opportunity for them. They got their logo right in the middle of all our promotional materials and raffle tickets. And it allowed us to provide a greater amount of exposure than we, as a smaller organization, are normally able to."

The donated money was spilt into two gift cards (one for $1,000 and one for $500), and tickets were sold by 40 volunteers, staff and board members. "It was the easiest thing in the world," says Linvill. "We spent almost no money — mostly just the cost of printing the tickets — and volunteers were happy to sell tickets for us. One took over 300 and sold them all. We raised over $10,000 our first year."

The biggest drawback she notes is the nature of raffles themselves. "A lot of people love them, but some people just don't like the concept of a raffle. And plans can struggle if a board member is one of those people."

But when there is solid support, a raffle can really boost an event's bottom line. "It's a great way to broaden your partnership with sponsors and leverage your sponsorship dollars," she says.

Source: Christine Linvill, Assistant Director, Family Support Line, Media, PA.
E-mail: Christine@familysupportline.org

$10,000 Sponsorship Idea

Here's a sponsorship idea you can use to generate an additional $10,000 or more: Identify 11 businesses each capable of contributing $1,000. Approach each and invite them to serve as sponsors of an event.

Ten of the $1,000 gifts will be used to generate $10,000 in needed revenue while the 11th gift will be used to underwrite benefits for each of the 11 sponsors (e.g., expenses that provide added value for the sponsors and make your project more successful).

ADDITIONAL STRATEGIES FOR SECURING SPONSORSHIPS

Vendors Keep Donor Recognition Costs Down

Create a sponsorship proposal that is specific to whoever you are approaching. Find out their past giving history, advertising habits, likes and dislikes and incorporate this information to create a proposal that is sure to win them over.

When development staff at Agnes Scott College (Decatur, GA) decided they needed financial assistance to underwrite a portion of their annual Tower Circle Dinner, they started looking close to home, reaching out to the college's existing vendors.

Vendors received a letter explaining the dinner's purpose (recognizing leadership donors to the college's annual fund) and a proposal that included a list of benefits for becoming a sponsor at various levels. Two vendors responded, one agreeing to sponsor at the $5,000 level and one at the $10,000 level, allowing sponsorships to cover 75 percent of the event's $20,000 costs.

In return for their sponsorship, the vendors were recognized on the college's website and in the dinner program. Two representatives from each of the companies were invited to the dinner, where they were thanked publicly in front of approximately 300 attendees.

Joanne Davis, director of the annual fund, says they take every opportunity to let alumnae know that the cost is being underwritten. "Alumnae appreciate the fact that the college does not have to pay the full cost of the dinner."

Source: Joanne Davis, Director of the Annual Fund, Agnes Scott College, Decatur, GA.
E-mail: jadavis@agnesscott.edu

Moving Billboards Drive Fresh Revenue Stream

Like many nonprofit organizations with declining grant funding and individual contributions, the Rockland County, NY, chapter of Meals on Wheels needed fresh ideas to generate revenue.

Then former board member and current fundraiser Nat Wasserstein realized an opportunity right under the organization's nose: placing advertising on the vehicles that deliver its meals. "Our trucks deliver 50,000 or so meals a week," making them moving billboards, Wasserstein says.

He suggested selling advertising space on the sides of those trucks.

This idea quickly snowballed into a second idea: Sell ad space on the shrink-wrapped covers of the meals themselves. With the interest of several, local small businesses — especially pharmacies, which offer vital products and services for the elderly — the group was able to increase revenue by thousands of dollars, Wasserstein says.

A similar advertising revenue stream is generating funds for the nonprofit Maltz Jupiter Theatre (Jupiter, FL). The theater company purchased a van during its 2009-2010 season to transport its youth touring company and the cast members of its Conservatory of Performing Arts outreach program. They designed two sets of magnets to affix to the van — one for each performance group. Then inspiration struck, says Jennifer Sardone-Shiner, the theater's director of marketing, and they soon were creating magnets for local sponsors.

Sardone-Shiner says the magnet program has exceeded the organization's expectations: "We have been getting a great deal of interest from potential sponsors, and many people have noticed our car. We feel that our sponsorship program offers a great opportunity for local businesses to support our community's nonprofit, regional theater and advertise while doing so."

Sources: Jennifer Sardone-Shiner, Director of Marketing, Maltz Jupiter Theatre, Jupiter, FL.
E-mail: jsardone@jupitertheatre.org.
Nat Wasserstein, Fundraiser, Meals on Wheels Programs & Services of Rockland County, Nanuet, NY.
E-mail: nat@lindenwoodassociates.com.

Advice for Securing Sponsorships

Robin offers the following advice when securing sponsorships:

- **Build a good committee.** "A strong volunteer committee is an organizational asset. It would be quite difficult for development professionals to structure sponsorship levels and benefits without the insight of those in the business community," says Robin.

- **Effective communication.** "Good communication with sponsors helps pave the way for future sponsorships. Make sure sponsors feel like their support was valued and that they truly helped. Robin says their website serves as a valuable tool for promoting events and sponsorships.

- **Build relationships.** "The development staff should find ways to constantly foster and build a relationship with each sponsor. Learn their names, preferences and anticipate their questions," she says.

ADDITIONAL STRATEGIES FOR SECURING SPONSORSHIPS

Theme, Sponsorship Key to Library Fundraiser

You've probably heard of the bestselling book "Eat, Pray, Love," but how about the fundraising event Eat, Play, Read to benefit a home to books, The Ferguson Library (Stamford, CT)?

"The event was our first ever fundraiser here at the library," says Communications Supervisor Linda Avellar. "We had recently completed a renovation of the main library and wanted to hold the event there, since many people in the community hadn't been in the building since the renovation. The concept Eat, Play, Read was a play on the popular book/film "Eat, Pray, Love," and was meant to be fun and a little whimsical. I think we achieved that with the evening we put together."

A dozen local restaurants and caterers donated food and set up tables to offer tastings. One of the town's major liquor stores donated wine, scotch and beer for tastings, as well as an open bar, reducing event costs tremendously. A jazz band played throughout the evening, while guests enjoyed a live auction and organized tours of the library. Those who participated in the tours were eligible for a raffle at the end of the evening. Avellar says, "It was a great way to get people around the building, and people were thrilled with the tours."

People also enjoyed the fact that the library, an elegant building with soaring ceilings and a grand staircase, was used as the venue.

Avellar says the event's intent was to be both a fundraiser and a friend-raiser. "We hoped to engage the entire Stamford community, especially those who might not be regular library users. We sustained a $1.2 million budget cut this year and were forced to scale back services and reduce hours system wide. Eat, Play, Read was an effort to raise funds and educate the community about what we do. On both accounts, we believe the evening was a big success."

The event raised approximately $100,000. Avellar says they had a robust response from individuals at every level of sponsorship. "We had 38 sponsors total, ranging from $500 to $25,000. The depth of the response was very encouraging." Indeed, it accounted for the majority of revenue raised.

Revenue was also generated through ticket sales, a live auction and a giving tree.

Source: Linda Avellar, Communications Supervisor, The Ferguson Library, Stamford, CT. E-mail: linda@fergusonlibrary.org.

Give would-be sponsors the opportunity to underwrite one component of an event or program — or the entire thing.

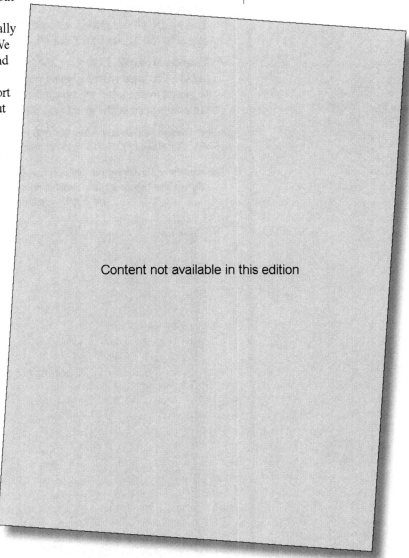

Content not available in this edition

The success of the Eat, Play Read event of The Ferguson Library depended in large part on sponsorship revenue. Shown here is the event-specific sponsorship form organizers used to raise donations of up to $25,000.

ADDITIONAL STRATEGIES FOR SECURING SPONSORSHIPS

Blueprint for a Half-million-dollar Fundraiser

The Spring For Schools Luncheon of the Bellevue Schools Foundation (Bellevue, WA) draws more than 1,000 guests and raises more than $500,000 each year. Marian McDermott, manager of institutional giving, shares elements central to the event's success:

✓ **Guests in the door**. "Our priority is getting guests in the door, so we don't sell tickets," McDermott says. Rather, a volunteer-run audience development committee recruits a body of table captains who, in turn, recruit the event's many attendees.

✓ **Corporate sponsorship.** In 2010, corporate sponsorship accounted for about a fifth ($117,000) of all funds raised at the luncheon. Bellevue benefits from major area corporations like Microsoft and Boeing, but McDermott says smaller businesses are major sponsors as well. "We actively recruit board members from the business community to stay as closely connected as we can," she says. "We are always making the case that good schools produce good employees and help attract good recruits from across the country and around the world."

✓ **Targeted giving campaigns.** The event's general fundraising efforts are bolstered by two targeted giving campaigns: The Angels matching campaign invites major donors to contribute $10,000 to a fund that matches gifts up to $1,000, while the Head of the Class campaign invites prominent community members — many of them high-profile business leaders — to pledge leadership gifts ($1,000-plus) in advance of the event. These gifts, recognized in the luncheon program, provide a powerful example for others to follow, says McDermott.

✓ **Coordinated ask.** Each year, the luncheon includes a suggested specific donation for guests. The most recent suggestion was $200 per guest. This amount is communicated to guests by the table captains, all of whom receive thorough training and preparation six weeks prior to the event (see illustration).

Source: Marian McDermott, Manager of Institutional Giving, Bellevue Schools Foundation, Bellevue, WA. Phone (425) 456-4199. E-mail: Marian@bsfdn.org

The success of the Spring For Schools Luncheon of the Bellevue Schools Foundation (Bellevue, WA) depends in large part on a small army of table captains. Foundation development staff carefully coach table captains to help them succeed using tools such as this handout.

Look for creative, non-traditional ideas — like asking sponsors to provide your event's waiters — as a way to involve sponsors in your event.

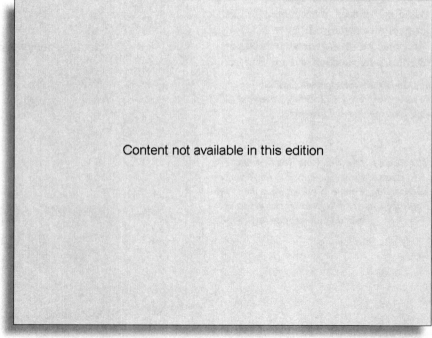

Content not available in this edition

ADDITIONAL STRATEGIES FOR SECURING SPONSORSHIPS

Reversing Corporate-sponsorship Model Increases Revenue

Typically, securing a corporate sponsorship means a nonprofit promises to promote its for-profit sponsors through its collateral material, press placements, special-event swag, multimedia advertising and so on -- with the costs and man-hours necessary to do so absorbed by the nonprofit organization. Conventional wisdom also dictates that the higher the sponsorship level a company agrees to, the more promotion it can expect from the nonprofit in exchange.

But when John Forberger, co-founder of 1in133 (Lambertville, NJ), which advocates for FDA-approved, gluten-free guidelines, sought sponsors for an awareness summit that his group hosted in Washington, D.C. last May, he knew that he would not be able to play by those traditional sponsorship rules; the nascent organization didn't have the funds or manpower to invest in those tried-and-tested avenues of promotion.

Instead, Forberger developed a reverse strategy for 1in133's sponsorship program. The organization offered three levels of sponsorship, but all sponsors were granted equal range to promote their association with the summit, whether they were sponsoring at the highest or lowest level. In other words, a small monetary sponsorship could still yield a disproportionately huge amount of exposure, but the sponsors would need to generate that exposure themselves.

Appealing mainly to companies that produced gluten-free foodstuffs -- an industry with plenty of room for growth -- Forberger says, "They all jumped immediately. It wasn't a hard sell for them to get involved with us." In the end, 1in133's list of summit sponsors included Bob's Red Mill, King Arthur Flour, Glutino, Enjoy Life Foods and Whole Foods.

Forberger knew the strategy would work because "whoever sponsored us was allowed to call out their sponsorship to all of their contacts, and manufacturers understood that this was a great tie-in for them." For example, "One manufacturer donated $133 [the lowest sponsorship level] and then, within 48 hours, sent out an e-mail to its entire online customer base, saying, 'For every package you buy of our food, we're going to donate x amount of the proceeds.'" In this way, 1in133 was also able to rake in revenue on the back end of its sponsorship deals at no extra cost.

Forberger says it was also key that his sponsors, relatively young and small corporations, were fluent at conversing with their customers via the Web. Thanks to their presence on such social-media platforms as Facebook and Twitter, sponsors could communicate directly to a targeted demographic in a matter of minutes and at no extra cost. "When someone backs you online, it just explodes," he says.

Source: John Forberger, Co-founder, 1in133, Lambertville, NJ.
E-mail: jforberger@oxfordcommunications.com.

Aim for Big-name Sponsors First

Although 1in133 allowed corporate sponsors equal opportunity to create tie-in promotions to its Gluten-Free Food Labeling Summit, no matter the monetary level at which they chose to sponsor the event, the nonprofit organization did invest time and resources into lining up its most well-known sponsor first.

Procuring Whole Foods as its first sponsor was crucial, says 1in133 Co-founder John Forberger, because "once you get the biggest people on board, the small ones will come along."

Sponsorship Tip

- When approaching a potential sponsor, explain that you want to give him/her the first opportunity to sponsor the entire event (or project) before inviting others. It saves time if you can get one business to cover the total cost rather than sharing it among a group of sponsors.